COMPLETE COURSE IN OIL PAINTING

Combined Edition—Four Volumes in One

COMPLETE COURSE IN
OIL PAINTING

Combined Edition—Four Volumes in One

by Olle Nordmark

BONANZA BOOKS · NEW YORK

This edition published by Bonanza Books,
a division of Crown Publishers, Inc.,
by arrangement with Reinhold Publishing Corporation

(R)

Photographs of materials courtesy of M. Grumbacher and Windsor & Newton

To Lasse, my wife

Contents

BOOK III

BOOK IV

Course

in Beginning

OIL PAINTING

Olle Nordmark

Introduction

The four books that comprise *A Course in Beginning Oil Painting* were conceived, written, and illustrated to fill a need for guidance in the achievement of sound craftsmanship. The instructions and exercises were planned to teach the student how to make full use of the information Nature herself offers with such a generous hand.

Learning how to paint a picture should properly begin with study of the art and methods of painting. Today, however, this is too often ignored in a frantic search for startling and exotic methods of painting. The need for sound craftsmanship in new methods, as well as in traditional methods, is too often forgotten. The laws that govern light, color, and the use of technical resources are the same for the realist as for the abstract painter.

To abandon craftsmanship at the beginning of study, in a mistaken quest for freedom, only retards the proper development of talent. Personality in painting grows from an intelligent search for a stable base from which flights into the realms of art can be safely launched. This series is a modest effort to help in charting the course.

Much in painting, especially in oil painting, is obscure even today; many problems still await sound solutions. But only time can prove whether or not new materials and methods are mere novelties rather than sound improvements.

The painter who is master of his material as well as of his ideas has, in his art, a personal means of expressing what is important to his individual development.

This course is intended to help the beginner achieve practical insight into the problems of painting with oil colors.

Olle Nordmark

Chapter 1

Before You Start Painting

In this book, the first in a series of four, I will explain as fully and simply as possible how to use oil colors rationally.

Painting in oil has almost unlimited possibilities. It lends itself so readily to varieties and combinations of techniques that it gives free scope to the inventiveness of the painter.

However, the painter who wishes to achieve brilliance of color from the first brush stroke through the last, as well as to retain it after a lengthy period of drying, cannot overlook certain basic rules of painting. The undisciplined use of palette and brushes usually results in sinking in tonality and after-darkening of pictures.

Before discussing basic rules, I would like to define some of the terminologies I will use. When I speak of the *palette* I do not mean just a piece of wood; I mean a chosen range of colors and hues, set up in a certain order—the arrangement and the color tones comprise the palette.

The particular shade of a color is the *hue*. The *chroma* is the degree of hue and saturation of each color, in other words, color intensity. Color *value* is the distribution of light and shade in a picture, often referred to as *chiaroscuro,* meaning clear-obscure. These are the attributes of color, not of individual colors.

Color in a picture is wholly dependent upon the quality of the color-tonality seen as a whole: the over-all color tone that sets one picture apart from any others.

Later I will discuss the palette in relation to its possibilities as a tone instrument, for the palette can be used and controlled by the painter in much the same way as the musician uses and controls his instrument.

Now, I would like to talk about the necessity of being prepared to paint. I am not in favor of making endless sketches in color for this leads to a final painting that is only an enlargement of a sketch. I am in favor of making fast idea-sketches. Do them in pencil, loosely

and freely; keep your mind relaxed so that you can record your impressions rapidly. To overcome any feeling that you are wasting expensive drawing paper on rough sketches, use the inside of envelopes or any other scraps of paper. Save your sketchbook for careful studies and pencil drawings. Remember that in this case quantity is more important than quality. Such small, fast idea-sketches stimulate the desire to start painting and, more important, solve the problem of what to paint before you begin.

Lay out your sketches in the sequence in which they were done. Several will catch your eye; from these select the one that has particular interest for you.

Keep this original intact. Do not attempt to work on it further for it will quickly lose the essence of its spirit, something that cannot be replaced no matter how much fine work is wasted on it.

The most expressive part of the sketch can be found by laying two "L" shaped strips of white paper over the sketch in such a way that they form a frame with an opening the same shape as your canvas. Move the frame about until you find the most interesting area of your sketch.

Now you are ready to start drawing on the canvas. Use a charcoal stick and the same direct, loosely drawn lines and forms characteristic of the sketch below. Working in this manner will develop style and real self-expression. You can earn freedom of expression only by trying to loosen the free flow of ideas, the beginning of all art.

The drawing reproduced here is one I did during my first summer of art instruction, when I was ten years old.

The soft green and blue summer landscape of my native province, Dalecarlia, in Sweden, has always attracted artists. Fortunately for me, the painter Gustaf Ankarcrona was one of those who came to work there during the summer months and he became my first teacher.

Three summers of study gave me an early start. The surrounding landscape was my art school, the visiting artists were my teachers.

Chapter 2

The Tools and Materials

I will list and briefly describe the tools and materials needed to start painting in oil. Expensive gadgets are not needed. They do not help the beginner. Buy good quality materials, consistent with the use you will make of them.

PAINTING SURFACES.

Linen Canvas. This is the most commonly used surface for oil painting, and the most satisfactory. It is also the most expensive.

Cotton Canvas. This is a good, cheaper substitute for linen. Only the heavier kinds: duck, sailcloth, and heavy sheeting are satisfactory for oil painting.

Both linen and cotton canvas are available primed and sized. Some shops carry stretched canvas ready for painting but most painters prefer to prepare the surface themselves. (See Book 4, the *Handbook,* for complete details.)

Tempered Masonite Board. This widely used modern material is excellent for outdoor painting because of its rigidity. Either face, smooth or rough, can be used after sizing and priming.

Pasteboard Prepared Panels. These are fine for small paintings. They are available with either a cotton canvas or a textured paper on one side. They are inexpensive and ready for use.

Oil Painting Paper. This is an economical and satisfactory canvas-substitute for students and practice painting. It is a canvas-like textured paper, primed to give it a white texture and grain similar to canvas.

TUBE COLORS.

Some colors are manufactured from earth pigments, some from artificial iron oxides, and some from dyes precipitated on fillers. Because of this, some are more chemically stable than others, and mixtures are more or less stable. Only a few of the important characteristics of color will be touched upon here. (See Book 4, the *Handbook,* for further details.) The earth colors include the siennas and ochres.

Burnt Sienna, a deep reddish brown, is made by treating raw sienna with intense heat.

Yellow Ochre is a natural pigment possessing special qualities of tone and feeling when mixed with other colors. It has no equal for landscape work and for producing elusive flesh tones.

Cadmium Yellow, light, and *Cadmium Yellow, deep,* are necessary to produce rich clear yellows and greens.

Cadmium Red, light, has its widest use in depicting the intensity of direct sunlight.

Rose Madder is equally useful in light or deep dark mixtures.

Alizarin Madder lends itself to cooler shades.

Cobalt Blue is one of the most durable blues and is stable in all techniques. It is particularly useful in underpainting because of its fast drying qualities.

Phtalocyanine Blue, or *Cyan Blue,* is a neutral blue, very useful in mixing dark greens and dark grays.

Ultramarine Blue is a very stable artificial pigment with a high saturation quality.

Viridian is a green that is dependable in all techniques.

Flake White, and *Cremnitz White* are basic lead carbonates, as is white lead. They are excellent white pigments poisonous in powder form, but in tubes they come ground in oil and can be handled with comparative safety.

Zinc White is an oxide of zinc and is nonpoisonous. It is somewhat transparent, useful as a mixing white, and safe with all colors.

Titanium White is a modern pigment and the whitest white. It is extremely opaque and not suitable for underpainting.

Half-White. This is a mixture prepared by the painter from equal parts of Zinc White and white lead. The white lead may be either Flake White or Cremnitz White.

PAINTING MEDIUMS.

The time-tested painting mediums are those containing a mixture of oil, varnish, and turpentine. Their purpose is to help apply the color to the painting surface and to speed up the drying and hardening. This rule applies to all painting mediums: use them sparingly.

Raw Linseed Oil is the most important medium to the painter. It must be of the finest quality and made specially for artists' use.

Damar Varnish, and *Mastic Varnish* are soft resins easily dissolved in turpentine.

Turpentine. The painter should use only high grade turpentines. I recommend Rectified Oil of Turpentine, and Gum Spirit of Turpentine; I consider the T&R brand, manufactured by Turpentine and Rosin Factors, Inc., of the highest quality.

Sun-Thickened Oil is an unsurpassed ingredient of painting mediums, which can be bought in art stores or easily made by the artist.

Intermediate Varnish, or *Retouching Varnish* is a lean mixture of damar varnish and turpentine.

Most mediums can be bought in any good art supply store. Some have to be mixed or prepared by the painter.

The painting mediums recommended in the painting exercises and descriptions of techniques in this series are:

Medium #1. A mixture of one part raw linseed oil, and one-and-one-half parts of turpentine. This is the thinnest medium, leaving only a slight sheen on the surface of the painting when the colors have dried.

Medium #2. A mixture of one part raw linseed oil, one part damar varnish, and one to one-and-one-half parts of turpentine. The varnish in this heavier medium produces a glossier surface and helps the color film harden, and dry faster.

Medium #3. A mixture of one part sun-thickened oil, one part damar varnish, and one-and-one-half parts of turpentine. The drying period is slightly longer and the gloss is a little higher than the #2 mixture. The pleasant enamel-like surface will remain after thorough hardening. It can be rubbed, when dry, with a soft rag to an even higher degree of glossiness.

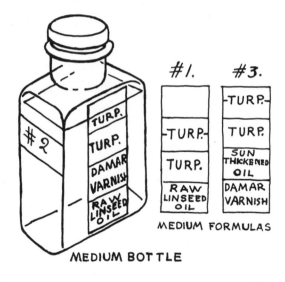

MEDIUM FORMULAS

MEDIUM BOTTLE

BRUSHES.

Three kinds of brushes are commonly used in oil painting: bristle brushes, sable hair brushes, and lettering brushes.

Bristle brushes are made in three shapes. *Brights:* flat and thin with short bristles. *Flats:* similar to brights but thicker and with longer bristles. *Rounds:* same length as flats, but round and coming to a pointed tip. The sizes are indicated by numbers ranging from 00 to 20.

Sable Hair brushes are made in brights and rounds, numbered from 00 to 20.

Lettering brushes are made of either sable

or ox hair. They have quite long hair, square at the tip.

The student needs only a few flats and brights selected from sizes 3 to 12; two or three bristle rounds, sizes 4, 9, and 12; two round sable brushes, sizes 9 and 10, and a lettering brush about ⅛″ wide.

Brushes are expensive; in order to keep them in top condition for as long as possible they must be washed carefully in soap and water at the end of each day's painting. The barbaric practice of standing them, bristle down, in

and shaping back into their original form with the fingers, and placed upright in a container to dry. They will then be ready for the next painting session.

PALETTE.

I refer here to the *carrier* of the colors, not the color range. This should be light and strong. The size and shape are matters of personal preference.

Bright	
Flat	
Round	
Lettering	

kerosene will ruin them in time. I have as many as thirty-five to forty brushes to clean, after a day's painting, and have never found it to be an unpleasant chore. Flax soap, a soft oil soap, or ordinary yellow naptha soap softened in water to a jelly consistency, is easily squeezed into the base of the bristle. Rinse and soap again until soap has been worked into all the paint. Then rinse in cold water until all the soap is removed. Never use hot water as it will destroy the brush. The rinsed brushes are wiped dry with a towel or rag, the bristles are "dressed" by squeezing

PALETTE KNIFE.

Mixing colors, cleaning the palette, scraping down areas in the painting are but a few of the uses of this versatile tool. I advise buying two, one straight, and one trowel-shaped.

PALETTE CUP.

There are any number of sizes, shapes, and designs of this implement whose sole function is to hold a portion of painting medium. It is clamped on the edge of the palette as shown in the photograph. It should be wide enough to permit easy dipping of the medium-sized brushes. For the larger brushes I advise a larger can standing within easy reach. Only a small amount of medium should be placed in the cup. Replenish as needed, but always clean out the residue left on the bottom before adding more medium. For this reason I prefer the straight-sided cup which makes the frequently needed cleaning easy. Cups with covers or sloping sides are hard to keep clean.

A word of caution about mediums: any medium left in contact with air will be unfit for color thinning in a few hours, and even more so after brushes have been frequently dipped into it, leaving a residue from many colors. Medium remaining in the cup must be thrown away. The oxidizing effect of the air, necessary to drying and hardening of the colors, is supposed to take place in the color film of the painting, not in the medium cup.

PAINT BOX AND EASEL.

While not essential, these items are practical. Some box-easel combinations are good for both studio and outdoor work. Select one according to personal taste and economy.

Chapter 3

Setting up the Palette

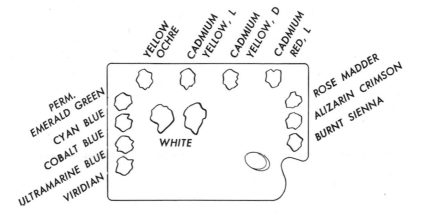

First look over the painting surfaces, colors, and tools; when you are sure that all is in readiness, set up the palette with colors and use them in the development of the idea conceived in your sketch.

In painting a picture, emphasis on a distinctive color scheme is the mark of a true personal style of expression in color and form.

A precise statement in color planned to express something in particular, whether mood, darkness, light, or any other desired effect, depends almost entirely upon the simplest and most direct handling of the colors set up on the palette.

The basic palette set up for this book has nine colors supported by three additional colors. With this palette's highly saturated range of hues we can reproduce, as nearly as is possible with pigments, the color of light as seen in the spectrum.

It is not necessary to imitate the color band in the spectrum; that would only limit usefulness and range. This palette is intended to help the student acquire a practical understanding of the laws of color, in mixtures, contrasts, and the two color factors: coldness and warmth. All of which, taken together, comprise the main features of color in painting.

The physical arrangement of the different hues should always be maintained in order to help the painter find his way over the palette quickly.

As a practical example, when painting outdoors at dusk, in moonlight, or even indoors in poor light, it is possible to paint in a minimum of light because the place of each color on the palette is fixed and can be found without hesitation or groping.

RANGE OF THE PALETTE.

The tube colors set out along the edge of the palette (*see illustration*), beginning at the lower left, are: Viridian; Ultramarine Blue; Cobalt Blue; Cyan Blue; Permanent Emerald Green; upper center: Yellow Ochre; Cadmium Yellow, light; Cadmium Yellow, deep; Cadmium Red, light; Rose Madder; Alizarin Crimson; and at the lower right, Burnt

Sienna. Placed further in on the palette is the white, generally in two places, one for the cold mixtures, blues, greens and violets; the other for the warm mixtures, yellows, oranges, reds, and browns. By this simple precaution of keeping the cold and the warm separated from each other, the mixtures can be kept clear and distinct, and accidental mixing of cold and warm colors can be avoided.

THE THREE SUPPORTING COLORS.

The Viridian, the Yellow Ochre, and the Burnt Sienna on the palette described above are the supporting colors. They are of great importance in oil painting. Because of their individual adaptability for creating depth in transparency, warm or cold silvery tones in light color schemes, and so forth, these three highly individual hues will strengthen or support other colors in "friendly" combinations without overemphasizing the values.

THE LIMITED PALETTE.

Sometimes a limited palette fulfills the needs of the contemplated color scheme. On the edge of the palette, mark off divisions with white chalk, one for each color to be employed, and print the abbreviated name of each color to be used (*see illustration*).

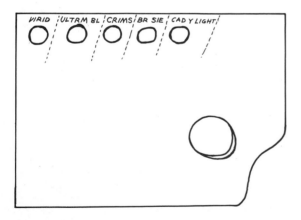

This system will keep the color scheme from slipping one's memory, and provide a memo of the palette used as long as it is needed.

THE THREE-COLOR PALETTE.

A simple palette can be set up with the so-called primary colors: blue, yellow, and red. These are primary only in the form of *pigments* such as oil paints. When mixed together they produce a more or less grayish black, depending on how close they come to being true *complementary colors*.

The exact opposite happens with the primary colors of *light*. Mixed together as light they produce *white light*.

The painter sees the colors of *light* and tries to reproduce them in *pigments*.

The scope of this book does not permit a lengthy discussion of color. This is an immense subject in itself. I must limit myself to helpful comments directly connected with specific palettes and with explanatory and practical exercises. However, before setting up the three-color palette for our mixing exercises, a short explanation of the colors of white light, as seen in the spectrum band, is necessary.

Sunlight, or white light, when projected through a prism onto a white surface, separates into nine colors. From left to right they are: violet, Ultramarine Blue, blue, blue-green, green, yellow-green, yellow, orange-red, and a red ending in a red darkness. This is the spectrum band.

The expression *primary colors* of light simply means the three principal colors of light as seen when projected through color filters. They are: a dark blue, a bright clear red, and a yellow-green. Combined in projection, their sum is white light. Projection of *pairs* of these primary colors is called *mixture by addition*. Where the projection beam overlaps, a mixture occurs which yields three more colors called *complementary colors:* light blue, purplish red, and yellow. These three complementary colors of light are the hues we will reproduce in pigments for the three-color palette employed in the color-mixing exercises.

THE THREE PRIMARY PIGMENTS.

To make the three hues, we use the following tube colors: Cyan Blue mixed with a small amount of white; Cadmium Red mixed with Alizarin Crimson and a little white to give the pigment a purplish cast; and Cadmium Yellow, light. Mixtures in pairs of hues from this palette are called *mixtures by subtraction*.

COLOR MIXING.

For a mixing surface, use a piece of window glass, approximately 12 inches square, placed on top of a piece of white paper.

A small amount of each of the three tube colors mixed as directed above, is placed on the glass, to form the three points of a triangle (*see illustration*). In the left corner the Cyan Blue,

Step one. Using the straight palette knife as the mixing tool, drag a portion of the yellow halfway down towards the blue, pull some blue up to meet the yellow and mix the two colors. Mix more of the blue into part of this medium green to get a blue-green and on the other side, more of the yellow until a clear yellow-green is achieved. Now, drag another part of the blue towards the red and the red towards the blue. From these, mix a section of purple. From part of the purple, mix a violet by adding more blue, and a deeper purple from additional red.

Mix red-orange from the yellow and the red. Divide this red-orange in half. Add more yellow to one portion to get a deep yellow; add

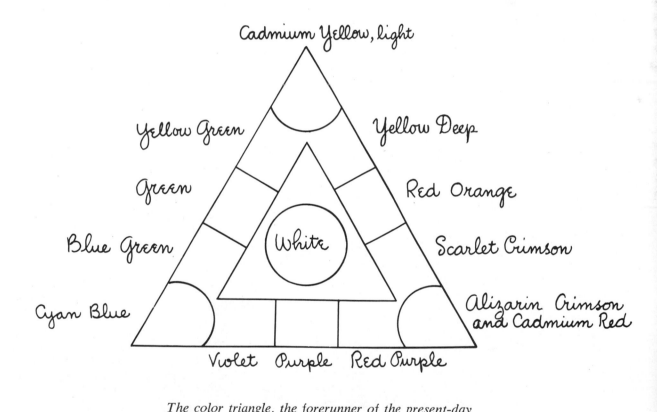

The color triangle, the forerunner of the present-day color wheel or circle, was first demonstrated by the French painter, Eugene Delacroix (1790–1863).

to the right Cadmium Red and Alizarin Crimson, at the top the Cadmium Yellow and in the center the white. This comprises *The Pigment Primary Palette.* The straight palette knife is used as the mixing tool. Be sure the knife is wiped clean before starting each new mixture.

more red to the remaining half to get a brilliant red.

Step two. Repeated use of complementary colors in painting will make the color scheme very tiresome and monotonous. To counteract such color monotony and to enrich the over-all tonality, add several colors of the same hue but with different characteristics and chromatic possibilities to the range of the working palette.

To paint effectively and rationally the painter must be aware of how cold and warm colors affect each other. It is important to understand that by juxtaposing cold and warm colors in painting, the cool color areas are brought forward and the warm colors retreat.

The greens are more or less middle-distance hues. They are also found in the middle of the spectrum band.

Cold blue brings things forward, violet re-

distance, depending in some degree upon surrounding contrasts.

If contrasted with warm greens, purplish red stays well in the foreground.

Division of color into cold and warm shades tends to build volume much more realistically than tedious shading which is a mere plastic rendering of *local colors*. Local colors are the colors of objects themselves as they would appear under an overcast sky.

The triangle in step one shows a yellow-green in the upper left; opposite and to the right, yellow, yellow deep, orange red and crimson. These are *warm colors*.

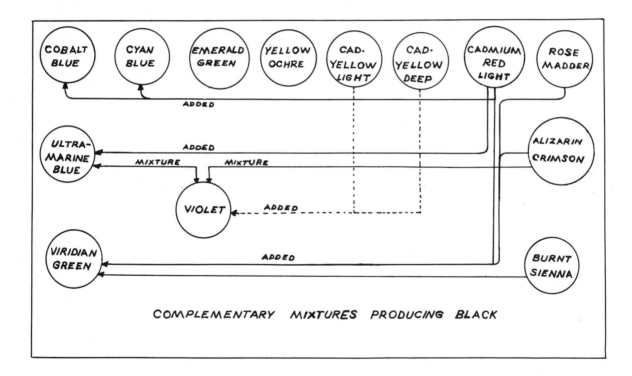

COMPLEMENTARY MIXTURES PRODUCING BLACK

cedes into the distance; bright yellows and yellow-greens will also draw back while a warm, darker green seems to remain between the foreground and the background.

Cold blue-green acts much the same as blue of a similar value.

Warm deep yellow, orange, ochre and Burnt Sienna are typical foreground colors, useful as contrast in foreground shadows. When juxtaposed with cool colors such as green foliage, they serve to bring the cool areas further forward. Reds and browns again are closer to the middle

In the lower left are blue and blue-green; at the base of the triangle, violet, purple, and purple-red. These are *cold colors*.

The effective use of cold and warm colors in separate areas is one of the main features of painting a picture.

Step three. In the center of the triangle there is a portion of white. Mix different shades from the three sides with some of the white in half-tone values. Addition of white will show all the changes taking place in each of the color combinations. When closely observed, silvery overtones can be seen in a variety of grays.

When the complementaries—blue, red, and yellow—are mixed together in full strength they form a black color by total subtraction or absorption.

We have now seen how combinations of complementary pigments produce blacks: and we know that the intensity of the blacks depends upon how close the colors are to being true complementaries. Several good blacks that are colorful and deep in value—towards a cool purple—come from mixtures of Viridian with Rose madder. The addition of a small amount of Burnt Sienna will warm the black without loss of intensity. Cobalt Blue mixed with Cadmium Red, light, with, perhaps, a small amount of Alizarin Crimson added, gives an exceedingly colorful black without a sooty effect. Cobalt Blue and

Burnt Sienna produce an asphalt-like black which is sometimes used to restrain color schemes on the verge of gaudiness. Viridian and Burnt Sienna combined makes still another black color.

Complementary blacks are related to all the colors on the full palette; many variations are possible, from colorful blacks, in cold or warm hues, to a neutral black color.

These highly saturated, deep-toned combinations of tube colors need to have a very small amount of Flake or Cremnitz White added to help in the drying-hardening process. A slight trace of the white showing in the mixture will in time become invisible.

All of the mixing exercises should be tried out in actual painting of a simple subject, drawing and painting in flat, simplified form, without shading. With "brush in hand" and a little patience valuable experience will be gained quickly.

Chapter 4

Painting the Picture

PAINTING THE PICTURE.

There are many ways to paint a picture. Different subjects can, of course, be painted in the same style and technique. But the painter's sensitivity to light, color, and other factors, often demands some deviation from personal style, a difference in approach from one subject to another, from one motif to another.

The beginning student, however, should select simple subjects that involve only two or three painting problems.

RED BARN

Here, for instance, is a simple landscape: a barn standing at the edge of a lake. The first step is a simple outline of the forms drawn in ink with a pointed stick.

The illustration was divided into two sections to show the undertoning on the left and the finished painting on the right. The sky and the strip of water were both toned in light yellow—Cadmium Yellow, light, and white, applied thinly in transparent color. A light tint of Cobalt Blue and white made the mountains and the tree group stand out in contrast with the yellow. Lighter blue over the middle ground, rose color over the rock, and a pink for the barn completed the undertoning.

After the tints were dry, painting began. The sky was done in crisscross brushwork and a warm airiness was created by mixing Rose Madder and white loosely in light strokes, letting the yellow tints show through. Long strokes of the same color partly covered the water with reflected light from the sky.

The foliage of the trees in the light was modeled with Permanent Emerald Green, Cadmium Yellow, light, and Cobalt Blue with white.

Yellow Ochre was used where light reflected from the ground, giving form to the trees in the areas turned toward the ground.

Cool green completed the water. The shadow in the tree group was done in dark blue-green strengthened with some Sienna. The bright top of one tree, painted in Cadmium Yellow and white, helped to bring more light into the foliage. Trunks and branches drawn in blue and Sienna completed the tree forms.

The blue and violet distance over the mountains had contrasts in variations of blue and yellow-greens.

The sunbleached red on the side of the barn, bordering on a blue-red, had the support of an undertone of pink. Strokes of red over a light tint of blue gave the roof a metallic sheen. The violet-black in the open window set the barn firmly into the green surroundings.

Middle green, Yellow Ochre, and blue, in slanting brush strokes, gave the grass freshness in contrast with the reddish blue and gray rock in the foreground.

A *dominant* in the general color scheme,

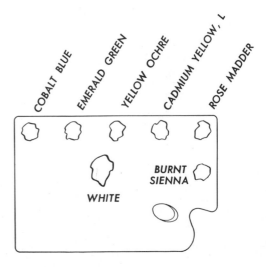

such as the red in the barn, can be rendered in colorful contrast against the whole of the picture. The violet shadow can also be utilized in the same way, but be sure to avoid a glaring, raw effect. A deliberate accent of a darker or lighter contrasting spot of color can be very effective.

Each step in painting a picture must look complete in itself. If each stage is carried out with this in mind the progress of the work will be easier to keep under control and the tonality of the painting will not fall apart at a later stage.

Note: In my description of the colors and color mixtures used in this painting, and all other paintings in this book, I have given the name of the color as it comes from the tube. This does not necessarily mean that the color, or color mixture, is to be used as is; it usually implies a certain modification, or graying, of the color mixture by the addition of the necessary amount of white. When a white is to be used in considerable amounts I have listed it as a component of the mixture.

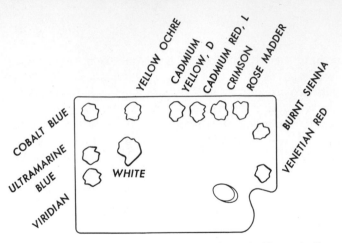

CEDAR

This is an exercise in painting a simple motif containing a very limited number of objects. It is also an exercise in painting a tree form. A cedar growing beside a stone fence is a typical landscape detail in many regions.

The painting began by covering the entire surface with a thinly painted-out tone of white with Cadmium Yellow, light. The cedar and stone fence were painted directly into this wet color without any previous drawing. Round brushes, dipped in the appropriate colors, were used to draw the shapes with rapid, firm strokes. No attempt was made at detailing or producing any special texture.

Because a cedar looks black when seen against the light, the general form of the foliage was painted in a semi-dark green made with Viridian, Yellow Ochre, and Cadmium Yellow, deep. This green was deepened with purplish shades by painting Viridian and Crimson into it. Shadows in this dark green were further strengthened and enriched with Sienna and Venetian Red. Cadmium Red and Cadmium Yellow, deep, add the extra brilliance of the reflected sunset-red.

The stone fence, standing in half-shadow, was painted a light blue-gray made of Cobalt Blue, Cadmium Red, light, and white. The reflected ground light was indicated by light strokes of Yellow Ochre. The optic light, or light from the sky, on top of each stone was painted with white, Rose Madder, and blue. Form-building shadows between the stones were drawn in Sienna deepened with Crimson.

The green used for the cedar, lightened with Ochre and Cadmium Yellow, was also used for the grass. It was scraped down with the palette knife to indicate the light over the distant field. The vista was closed with hills on the horizon drawn in light strokes of Ultramarine Blue and Zinc White.

The sky was finished in long slanting brush strokes of white with Rose Madder. It was made stronger toward the horizon, darker at the top and shaded lighter downward. Cobalt Blue and white in a semi-opaque mixture were lightly brushed into the underlying rose and yellow.

The problem of painting a motif that has a limited number of objects was solved by the proper juxtaposition of the colors in cold and warm tones. The feeling of depth was created by the contrasts in color and their position in the form.

To preserve intensity and clearness of hue when painting the picture, the following reminders are of the greatest importance:

(1) To avoid darkening and thereby lowering the tonality of the picture, paint only with clean brushes and a clean palette. Have enough brushes to keep color opposites apart—that is, don't pick up a red pigment with a brush you have used for green. Clean the medium cup at intervals, and use only fresh medium, not dirty leftovers.

(2) Mix only two colors in any one spot. Move to another spot on the palette for additional colors. Avoid all lengthy brushing or mixing. Learn to let the colors mix on the canvas rather than deadening the tone by too much mixing on the palette.

(3) Avoid overdoses of oil in mediums and lack of air or light in drying of a picture. Both cause after-yellowing of the colors.

(4) To avoid muddy tones do not mix colors that cancel each other out.

WINTER, Dalecarlia, Sweden

Half-white and Rose Madder were loosely mixed together and the entire canvas covered thinly, in a half-covering fashion. The general color of the houses, Burnt Sienna, was distributed into this coating with a stiff brush. Accents in Ultramarine Blue, used mostly as a shadow color, gave form to the logs.

Another light overpainting of the sky in white and Yellow Ochre was followed by white and Ultramarine Blue. The last two coats were painted out in crisscross brushwork unifying the three hues in such a way that a leaden gray, without atmospheric characteristics, was avoided. The same color treatment was employed in painting the snow on the roofs and on the ground, except for a more pronounced bluish cold and a barely visible touch of violet on the roofs' shadow side and beneath the buildings.

Crimson and Burnt Sienna in light shadings, and some additional drawing with blue shaped the logs and the architectural details.

Snow painted into the crevices of the walls added a frosty touch to the wood. Only a sharpening up of the drawing here and there was necessary to complete this example of a typical painting in cold and warm.

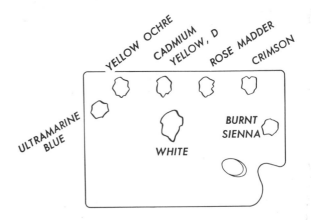

LANDSCAPE

For this painting exercise I selected a motif set in the early morning sunlight when light and shade are simplified and interesting. In the early hours, when the sun is still low, it is possible to work with a few relatively subdued color tones without losing intensity of light and color.

The palette for this painting was restricted to eight colors arranged in the following order: Viridian Green; Cobalt Blue; Yellow Ochre; Cadmium Yellow, light; Cadmium Red, light; Alizarin Crimson; Burnt Sienna; and Zinc White, which was placed near the center below the Ochre.

The painting medium was a mixture of one-part raw linseed oil and two-and-a-half parts of gum turpentine shaken together. A small quantity, one ounce or less, is more than sufficient for a painting of this size (12 by 16 inches). Like any kind of thinner it must be used very sparingly.

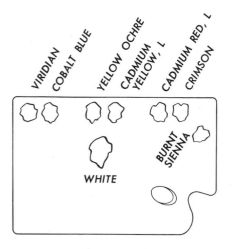

Step 1. Each separate form was distinctly outlined with a hard (3H) pencil which eliminated much of the guesswork in controlling color and color value.

I began with the darkest colors of the motif, the sienna-colored gable and porch siding. This approach is a great help in establishing the color values throughout the painting. Contrasted against this warm, rich color tone, the cooler colors quickly register true values. Next, I painted the blue roof of the porch in Cobalt and red, the green shutters in Cobalt and Ochre, and then the purplish darkness in the windows, thus establishing the first color notes in the painting.

It should be noted here that the listing of colors used to paint any given area refers to mixtures of the colors mentioned, controlled by the addition of white.

The dark shadow across the foreground was painted in a deep shade made of Viridian, Ochre and some blue. The trunks of the two trees were painted a blue-gray mixed from Cobalt Blue and Sienna. A lighter shade of the same color marked the strip of highway behind the house.

Painting of the sky began at the top with Cobalt Blue lightened with white, moving downward around the two clouds. Then, starting from the outlining of the mountains below, a light shade, made of white, Crimson, and a small amount of Ochre, was painted upward, meeting and mixing with the blue and gradually lightened with white to produce a soft passage between the two colors. The clouds were underpainted with the shade of the color along the horizon and the mountains painted with the same shade mixed with blue.

Step 2. An undertone of semi-transparent yellow-green mixed from Viridian, white, Cadmium Yellow, and some Yellow Ochre was painted in the area between the highway and the foreground shadow.

The practice of using an undertone in establishing the main areas of a painting is helpful and practical. From the first brush strokes the

development of the color scheme becomes easier and faster.

The background trees, the tree near the house and the top of the tree in the foreground were painted in an undertone of Cadmium Yellow with white. The warm gray color over the house wall—Sienna and white—was painted next. By adding some blue to that color, the foundation could be finished in a darker gray. Light Ochre window shades and the brick-red chimney completed the second step.

Step 3. Viridian, blue, and Cadmium Yellow were mixed to a blue-green shade and painted in flat modeling on the bushes at each side of the house. Some of the yellow undertoning shows as a top light on the bushes and will serve as a useful indication in the final stages of painting.

A gray-green was painted above the foreground shadow in slanting brush strokes, simulating a bank of thick grass. Viridian, yellow, and blue were mixed to a warmer, brighter shade of the undertone and painted above the gray-green bank; this tied the dark shadow to the rest of the color scheme.

The remaining foliage of the foreground tree was covered with a semi-transparent green of white and Viridian warmed up slightly with yellow; this served as a basic color contrast in the shaded lower parts of the tree.

Step 4. (*See color spread.*) The lower branches were shaded darker by brushing soft spots of Ochre and Cadmium Yellow into the green. This divided the foliage into three distinct values.

Near the base of the trunk three rectangular flat stones were painted a light gray over the darker shadow to bring the geometric forms of the house into harmony and balance with the foreground. Simple flat shadows were painted in blue-green, in half-covering brush strokes, on the tree near the house. Below, the bushes were made deeper in color in the shadow with Viridian and Crimson.

The light-colored trees along the highway were divided into individual groups of trees by light strokes of semi-covering blue.

Step 5. (*See color spread.*) The finishing stage began by modeling the siding of the gable and porch with horizontal brush strokes. A light, transparent mixture of Sienna and white was used for this, giving the siding both texture and form.

The orange curtains were added, using a mixture of Crimson and yellow. Blue-gray shadows were added inside the windows, under the window sills and the shutters. The shadow line of the foundation followed. Note the reflected light at the ground line.

The details of the shutters were added with a lighter green than the shutter green. The chimney was then finished, and the white trim added. A touch of deeper darkness was added between the curtains, completing the finishing touches on the house.

Cool bluish light was painted over the top of the bushes; a stronger blue over those in the shade of the tree at the right. This group was given additional depth in the shadow with single brush strokes of Crimson with blue.

The trunk of the tree was painted with a dark blue made of Cobalt and Crimson, with white graying the mixture slightly. This related the trunk to the bushes around it.

By the simple expedient of changing to another kind of red in the shadow color, color precision in contrast is clarified.

An airy blue-green was painted over the shadows of the foliage of this tree, well inside the shadow forms. A lighter green made of Viridian, blue, yellow, and white was placed in between. This is a cool, half-covering green which represents the light over the tree. The yellow undertone is left to show around the brush strokes, contouring them. This reflected color creates the volume of the whole tree. Extra strength was added to the reflected light from below by a few strokes of Yellow Ochre in the lower shadows.

Crimson, white, and Ochre in the clouds were applied with an airy softness. The same light touch was used with the violet-blue over the mountains.

Long strokes of Ochre gray-green, allowing the darker green undertone to show through, and other lighter lanes of bluish gray-green brought out the cool light over the ridges in the open field.

Touches of cool gray light were then applied to the trunk of the foreground tree. I mixed some light green from Viridian, white, and small amounts of Ochre and Cadmium Yellow to make a warm shade. I prepared a small heap, enough to paint the whole tree without remixing. This was applied in small leaf-like blobs placed far enough apart to allow the different undertones to activate the green by contrast.

The small trees in the distance were further individualized by soft shadows in blue and in airy blue-greens. A sheen of optic blue over the highway and the distant mountains finished the painting of this landscape exercise.

TEMPERA WHITE IN COMBINATION WITH OIL COLORS.

Egg tempera has been used for centuries as the binder of pigments in painting on wood panels. When painters discovered that the egg could be emulsified with oil or varnish, the dawn of oil painting was at hand.

The fifteenth century Italian and Dutch painters made extensive use of tempera white in their work. When looking at the Hollanders' work it is exceedingly hard to tell where they have used the tempera. The fusion between the tempera and the oil-color film is complete and invisible.

The beginning of the eighteenth century saw the end of tempera. Notoriously unstable pigments, such as Asphalt Brown came into wide use. This ruined not only the paintings themselves, but much of the entire technique of painting in oil.

In the first part of the nineteenth century there was an attempt to return to sound methods of oil painting. The egg emulsion used by Hans von Marée (1837–1887) brought back one of the most stable methods of oil painting—tempera underpainting combined with resinous oil-color overpainting. In feeling and expression von Marée's paintings are very close to our contemporary style.

WORKSHOP TABLE

This motif, showing the use of three constants painted in a triad of color tones, was arranged with three paper bags containing dry colors: Cadmium Yellow, deep, on the left, then Permanent Emerald Green, and on the right, Crimson Red. Dull, dark-green shadows were painted into the folds of the paper bags, to contrast with the bright color-dust on the outside.

Three hard-surfaced objects were placed between the bags, to relieve monotony and to create contrast between soft and hard light.

Blue-gray cardboards provided a cool background to the right and acted as a cold shadow against the sunlit left side. This side was painted in light yellow and rose; the light yellow

and rose was also used over the gray-blue shadow at the right edge of the sunny side, and over the table.

The soot-blackened oil lamp behind the red bag established the necessary color balance.

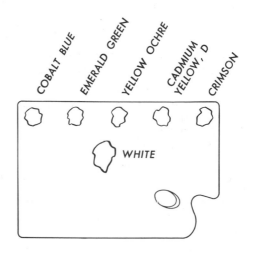

Chapter 5

The Imprimatura

This is a transparent color coat used as a canvas tone base to provide contrast between the canvas base and the painting to follow. For example, before painting the pinkish shades of the nude body the canvas is given a warm greenish imprimatura, soft and mild in feeling and light enough to let the ink drawing show through clearly. Or, for contrast with the greens in a landscape, the canvas could be given a rose-gray tone, not too cold or warm and somewhat silvery in feeling. The enhancement of general color or tonality by such static contrast helps to enrich the total color scheme of the completed painting.

The imprimatura is sometimes shaded from a dark to a lighter value. This effect can be achieved in a variety of ways. Some painters place a piece of tissue paper over the canvas and rub the area that is to be lightened. When the tissue paper is lifted a certain amount of paint sticks to it and lightens that area of the imprimatura. Wiping out with a rag is not recommended because it always produces a numb, dead-looking surface. Scraping with the trowel knife, however, does just the opposite; it leaves a lighter color that is full of life.

All painters use the scraping method to some degree. Rembrandt, for instance, might, at times, have scraped off as much as he laid on in order to produce the scintillating color areas in his paintings. The effect produced is called *vibrato*, vibration of color.

Scumbling, another method of bringing out vibrato, is accomplished by pressing slightly sideways on a flat brush so that the bristles leave a trail of color on the high spots of the canvas or color texture. This technique has been widely used with tempera or oil color in all periods of painting.

Before attempting to use these methods in a painting, the student would be wise to try them out on odds and ends of canvas or panel board until both the techniques and the effects they produce are understood.

When painting in optic gray, discussed later, such devices as shading or lifting of the imprimatura are rarely used.

OIL IMPRIMATURA or GLAZING MEDIUM.

This is mixed from equal parts of full strength damar or mastic varnish, and turpentine. To this mixture add a small amount of sun-thickened linseed oil to make the medium flow smoothly. If it is necessary to thin out the mixture, a very small amount of turpentine may be added.

This medium sets and dries rapidly, therefore it must be applied quickly in order to avoid ugly lapses in the imprimatura, which is laid on in one direction in a rather streaky fashion. The loose, uneven appearance of this undertoning can be used constructively throughout the painting of the optic gray.

After a day of drying, the oil imprimatura is ready for the tempera-white overpainting.

Chapter 6

Painting in Oil Tempera

A flat white enameled dish, or a dinner plate, can serve as a practical palette for the tempera painter.

Only a few brushes are needed for the tempera-white underpainting: a medium-wide one and a smaller one for detail. Because tempera colors become insoluble if allowed to dry out, it is important to rinse brushes occasionally during the painting period. When work is com-

pleted, brushes and palette must be thoroughly washed with soap and water and then rinsed in clear water. Otherwise hardened paint will make them useless.

Painting shadows with transparent color and using more-or-less opaque, light tones over dark backgrounds, results in a tempera painting in gray that has strongly defined light and shadow values. These can be varied at will to

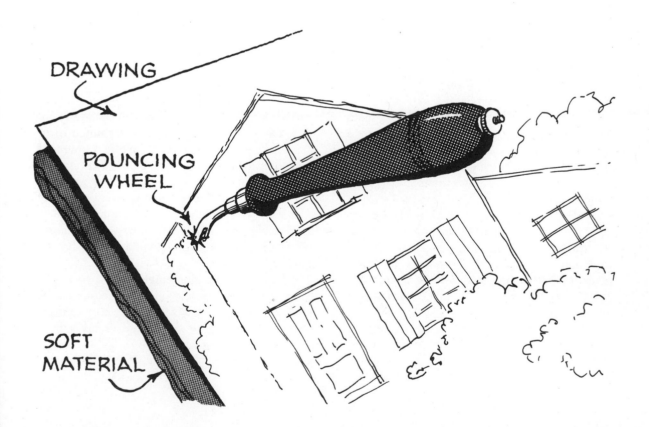

DRAWING

POUNCING
WHEEL

SOFT
MATERIAL

emphasize either of the two values, or to produce a general softening of the whole painting. This type of underpainting is called *Painting in Optic Gray,* which will now be described in detail.

PAINTING IN OPTIC GRAY.

The following description of this underpainting method should help the student to make effective use of tempera in oil painting.

However, before going further, I do want to make it understood that this venerable method is not bound to any old-style realism, round modeling, or minuteness of detail, quite the opposite. It can be as helpful to extremely modern painters as it was to those of the Renaissance.

Before starting to draw, the primed surface is lightly rubbed down with a rag dipped in tempera mixed with water. This prevents the ink lines of the drawing from crawling, that is, shrinking and creeping over the surface.

A charcoal stick can be used to draw directly on the primed surface; or the drawing can first be made with a pencil on a piece of tracing paper and then transferred.

When using the transfer method, the lines of the pencil drawing are perforated with a needle held in a wooden handle or with a pouncing wheel (*see illustration*). To ensure open perforations and to prevent ripping, the perforating is done on top of a soft material such as a double-folded blanket. The perforated drawing is then placed in position over the canvas and the holes dabbed with powdered charcoal or a charcoal stick can be run along the perforated lines. In either case rub the charcoal in with a rag. This method is called *pouncing* or transfer of a drawing.

The charcoal drawing on the canvas is inked with a square-tip lettering brush, or the pointed end of a small brush-handle, and black waterproof ink diluted with a small amount of water. The inked drawing should be as simple as possible—merely an outline of the subject plus an occasional important detail and indications of the main areas of light and shadow.

If the transfer method has been used, the tracing paper drawing can be further developed by filling in the shadow areas with slanting lines and emphasizing the light areas with chalk. The drawing then gives a strong impression of light and shadow thus becoming a helpful guide to painting.

When hard and dry, waterproof ink is impervious to oil color and to the water in tempera colors. The ink outline on the canvas must, therefore, be completely dry before any painting can begin.

The canvas with its ink drawing is given a coat of transparent oil color in a light, warm brown or a dark, purplish red. When this oil imprimatura is dry another thin streaky coat of tempera white is applied.

Before this thin tempera coat is dry, modeling of the form in tempera white is begun. The light areas are painted first; highlights are added as the work proceeds and the highest lights are painted last. Care is taken not to run too far into the passage between light and shadow.

The oil imprimatura can be painted over the darkest areas to create depth. However, overdoing this will give the painting a general feeling of heaviness.

When the tempera white painting seems to be developed far enough, it is permitted to dry and then given a thin coat of in-between varnish. When the varnish is dry painting in oil colors can begin.

The following illustrations show two stages in an optic gray underpainting. The subject is the head of a young woman, but the principles involved hold true for any subject in any light. *(Continued on page 43)*

One. A thin layer of tempera white has been rubbed over the surface and the charcoal drawing has been inked. The warm-brown imprimatura has been laid over the ink drawing and another thin streaky coat of tempera white has been applied over the completely dried imprimatura. The uncovered edges show the transparency of the thinned tempera white.

Two. The tempera white modeling was started while the tempera coat was still wet and the modeling has been developed just about enough. Notice that the flat, transparent middle tone or passage has been retained through this final stage of the optic gray painting. The painting has been allowed to dry and is now ready to receive a coat of varnish before painting starts.

PAINTING OVER THE OPTIC GRAY.

This begins with the general color of the light on the hair and face of the model. However, care must be taken not to run this light color too far into the gray passage, which is a middle shadow tone that carries over to the light area and is important to the sculptural form of the subject. The darker shadows are laid in warm, transparent color in flat painting, as was done in painting the light areas.

Next in importance are the eyes, nose and mouth. In order to give the face life and likeness, these features should be finished as nearly as possible early in the painting.

The background is also brought to an advanced stage by giving attention to the colors that must contrast attractively with the figure when the painting is completed.

Ears, cheeks, and lips now receive their important rosy coloring. This is also the time to put warmth in the light areas and to do further development of the shadows, again in transparency.

Final painting of the shadows, and warm, soft yellow highlighting of the light areas is undertaken next. Reflected lights are warmed with Ochre, adding Burnt Sienna on the parts turning downward. Bluish light is applied in the shadow areas that are turned upward, such as on the shoulder. The warm and cold colors were used as just described because warm light is reflected into shadow areas from below and cold light is reflected into shadow areas from above.

This procedure has been dealt with in the most general terms in order to indicate to the student what he himself should observe closely. The law of reflected light is the same for any object, anywhere.

Strong coloring is left to the last when everything seems to balance in light and dark, cold and warm.

GLAZING.

This is attempted only over lighter underlayers. It must be remembered that all transparency in painting means a certain lowering and darkening of the color. Too many glazing coats, especially in complementary colors, end in total darkness, a sort of luminous black.

The old masters' glazing methods, such as Titian's "30–40 glazes," or even Rembrandt's glazed darkness, are not for us; we live in an era of immediate expression. Few painters can face the tedious procedure, the difficult days, months, and even years of hard work on a single painting that these glazing methods involve.

ALLA PRIMA PAINTING.

In this "wet in wet" painting method the color is laid on rapidly into wet underlayers until the painting is completed. The phrase is from the Italian expression meaning "at once."

BACK YARD

Once I had made a definite decision to paint this scene, certain preliminary work was necessary.

First a charcoal outline sketch was made on the canvas. Then, on a palette, I pre-mixed small heaps of the principal local colors, enough for the entire painting.

On a second palette, I mixed colors for the general light and shadow areas. On a piece of painting paper I tested colors for the foreground and background greens, the light and shadow over the grass, the ground, the street at the right, and the gray siding of the shed.

When I was satisfied with my tests I started work on the canvas by laying down the undertoning. I used light yellow for the undertoning of the sky, Ochre for the large center building, and light gray for the shed.

Although most of the painting exercises shown elsewhere in the book were done on 12 by 16 inch painting paper, this picture was painted on a stretched canvas 16 by 24 inches. Through my tests I had obtained a preview of the color scheme showing all the basic tones. This made actual painting much easier and speedier for many color problems had already been solved. The pre-mixed colors were now used in developing the forms on the canvas. Light scraping of the colors with the palette knife was followed by detail drawing in Rose Madder with a lettering brush. The painting at this stage has the appearance of half-lights and half-shadows.

The second stage began by deepening the shadows and lightening the areas in direct sunlight with fairly thin color coats. Stronger color notes in the dark areas and highlighting in the light areas gave the painting a stronger tonality.

The warm, reflected light on the foliage was painted next. Other areas were softened by additional scraping to achieve transparency. The subject now emerged in full color, controlled by this simple, direct method of painting.

The use of Venetian Red and shades of Sienna brought the dominating brick wall, silhouetted in the center, into harmony against the light blue of the sky.

The gradual development of the picture continued as the loosely painted beginning was strengthened, systematically moving from one area to another. Painting in cold and warm tones, I did not commit myself to anything final in any part of the painting at this stage, but brought all elements toward completion together.

The final stage of painting proceeded quickly, unhindered by repainting and overpainting which might have been necessary if I had completed any one element before another. The

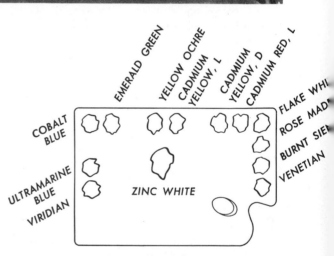

sky was finished, a glint of light was added here and there in the thick color, some added detail was drawn in Sienna, Rose Madder, and blue, to emphasize form and depth, and the picture was complete.

I painted this subject from an upstairs window, finishing each stage of painting in one day before there was too much change in the light. Three hours of work every day, from nine to noon, was the limit of fairly constant light. By working too long and too strenuously on this type of painting, heavy in detail, there is great danger that both the light in the painting and the general tone will become indecisive due to the great difference in light from day to day.

Medium #2 was used for thinning.

ERASURE WITH TEMPERA WHITE.

This is the quickest and safest way to correct large areas in a fresh painting. The areas to be corrected or changed may be too dark, poorly balanced in color, the wrong color, or wrong for a number of other reasons. Painting over such areas could further unbalance the picture, for the new colors would probably mix with the wrong old ones, or the underpainting effect might be lost.

The procedure for making corrections with tempera white is a simple one. If the fresh oil colors are heavy or dark, they are scraped off the area to be corrected, then tempera white is applied and allowed to dry thoroughly before overpainting is resumed. If the color is light and not too thickly applied, the tempera white is painted directly into the wet oil color. An hour of drying time is usually sufficient to permit painting over the erasure.

The illustration, representing a landscape in the rain, shows the places erased with the help of tempera white. This picture has approximately the same color scheme as the "Red Barn" in chapter four, but it is slightly grayer in tone. The same palette was used, and the underpainting of yellow, blue and rose is the same.

Chapter 7

Light Changes the Object

Whenever light strikes an object from a different angle an entirely different effect is produced. Light, or the lack of it, changes the values of light and shadow areas and therefore the object itself seems to change.

Seen against the light, form seems to shrink. In flat frontal light, form retains its shape.

Buildings of light color appear to have little weight in frontal light, but against the light they change to solid, heavy masses of shadow color. The silhouetted shadows all seem to be of nearly the same hue, a sort of violet brown, like a mixture of Rose Madder, white and Burnt Sienna. Sometimes, reflected blue and yellow light from surrounding areas enriches the dark quality of this type of shadow.

Light affects form in many ways. For example, try painting the same motif close up, then at a distance, and then after that use a smaller area of the motif for a third painting. There will be surprising differences even though the same light shown on each motif. It will be all the more obvious if a simple subject is chosen and the form and light are simplified. This is a very valuable exercise in learning to understand the behavior of light.

The familiar set of "memory colors," such as blue for the sky, green for grass, and brown for the road, are all local colors and sometimes subject to radical changes under different conditions created by light, atmosphere and distance.

Distance and atmosphere have the ability to change colors. The same silhouetted shadow that is warm in the fore or middle ground will change to a cooler violet, getting bluer as it recedes into the far distance. For example, an autumn-yellow tree in the foreground if seen in far distance through a bluish mist, would appear to be a rose color. A green tree will take on a hue of blue and violet when seen from far away.

When Claude Monet, the French Impressionist, began his famous series of Poplars, Haystacks, and Cathedrals, he recorded the successive changes of light and color in his subjects. Using several canvases for each subject, he painted on one canvas as long as the light was constant, then passed on to the next canvas as the light changed. By starting at exactly the same

time each day that the light and weather were consistent, he succeeded in producing a series of heroic works. He was able to paint only for brief moments on each canvas but the magnificent result of his work made a profound impact on our technical knowledge of oil painting.

DARKNESS AND DEPTH IN PAINTING.

Depicting darkness in painting is generally successful only after the painter has acquired some understanding of the nature of darkness itself.

The darkness over a landscape is quite different from that of a dark room. The many kinds of moonlight are again entirely different. Black alone will not express darkness, it will express only the dark local color of a dark object. The darkness around this object is the obscure luminous stuff we call darkness, which is lack of light. Exceptionally good examples of painted dark are found among the works of Titian, Rembrandt, Correggio, Caravaggio and other artists of olden times.

Titian's glazed darkness (said to be as many as thirty to forty glazes one over the other) gave the dark in his paintings a mysterious quality, still undefinable and obscure today. Exactly how he arrived at this perfect antipode to light, or what technical procedure he used, is not entirely known. His thorough knowledge of the complexity of complementary colors gave him the exact sequence of his many overlaid color transparencies, the glazes.

Rembrandt, the other master of the painted dark, created the depths of gloom by using a rich golden light as the complementary opposite. The heavy shadows that sometimes lurk in his pictures, or the hues of the intangible glow of the soft, undefinable darkness, are still wonders of painting. When his picture was painted to a certain degree of finality Rembrandt overlaid his glazing color and then promptly scraped it off with something like a spatula made of horn. The final glazing, or glazings, completed the vibrating dark which is the mark of this master.

Correggio and Caravaggio gave us a different definition of the dark and obscure. By contrasting a flat darkness against a strongly modeled, sculptural light, their paintings leave us with an impression of a deep dark, of a more directly felt black color.

Most of their works show much of the same tendency toward flat areas of blackness, in opposition to Rembrandt's many degrees of different depths of darkness.

In contemporary painting, the night sky and the sunlit sky have several problems in common: first, how to paint and preserve the luminous depth to keep it from getting lost in overpaintings; and secondly, the color problem.

The northern and the southern skies are diametrically opposite in color as well as in position. The eastern and the western parts of the sky link them together in color. To describe, or to prescribe for painting, the dark blue, blue-black or violet of the night sky is very close to impossible. The summer night with its feeling of warmth in the sky is probably the hardest sky to reproduce in color.

Painting in dots or curved lines of different hues, each hue separately painted over the entire canvas, will create the illusion of a transparent dark of considerable depth. For this technique, an undertoning in a straight thin glaze is applied over the whole of the canvas. The color tone should be able to hold the whole tonality together without being heavy in feeling or deadening the final color value of the night darkness. All parts of the painting must, of course, be followed up in the same style, in curved or straight lines, dots, or a brushwork invented on the spur of the moment.

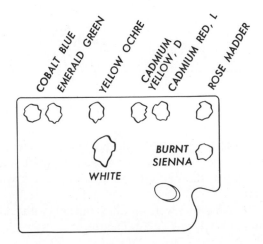

COBALT BLUE EMERALD GREEN YELLOW OCHRE CADMIUM YELLOW, D CADMIUM RED, L ROSE MADDER

WHITE BURNT SIENNA

I advise students to try out this "calligraphic" painting technique on several different problems. Use colors near each other in value but not so close as to approach being complementary. Great care must be taken to keep the dots, or the lines, far enough apart to avoid closing up the texture of the color surface and causing the painting to become opaque and heavy looking. Thus, painting a warm blue summer night, which is otherwise almost impossible, can be successfully accomplished.

The variations on this technical procedure, improvisations on entirely different problems, can be tried out and solutions found to catch and hold the elusive darkness on the canvas.

The degree to which a color is deep or distant, the quality of its darkness in the shadows, or the richness of its tone, are all closely knit together in a picture. All are equally responsible for the successful outcome of the painting.

The creation of depth and distance by the juxtaposition of various elements of the composition were described earlier.

How far this should be carried out is entirely personal and depends upon the degree of the relative reality of the painting. Contrasting with flat dominating parts, an over-extended depth in perspective can be helpful in balancing the color values from the foreground into the distant background.

Later in this series I will return to the problems related to darkness and depth.

HOUSES BY THE SEA, Scandinavia

This painting was executed primarily in local colors: the colors of the objects themselves as seen under an overcast sky. They were placed against each other in subdued hues. Without sunlight and its strong shadow, local colors stand out clearly almost devoid of the complexity of light reflected from other colors.

Linear perspective of the houses was held to a minimum and color was divided into the two values of light and shadow. Modeling was also held to a minimum to bring out a certain naive simplicity.

Variations of color in the sky were painted mostly in pink and shades of Cadmium Red, Cobalt Blue, and white; a light shade of Yellow Ochre brought warmth to the clouds. The upper left corner shows a patch of the blue sky.

The sea was painted Cobalt Blue and Viridian, the waves slightly deeper in color. Light strokes reflected the sky color over the water and the foam-crested waves were finished with white.

The house with the white triangle on the gable had a body color of Ochre and Sienna and a gray stone footing. The other two buildings were paneled and painted red brown; tiled roofs in Ochre and red provided a stronger note against the blue sea.

The fence was in red brown; the rocks gray with shades of red and blue and spots of green moss.

Shadows in the birch trees and the foliage of the darker trees differed only in being a bluer or greener blue-green. Light green with Ochre and white, slightly browned, dressed the birches in summer colors.

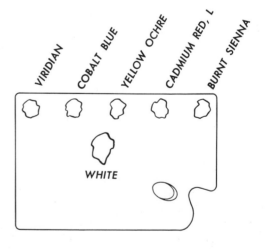

The grass around the houses and under the birch trees are the strongest and brightest spots of green; the darkest blue-green is in the windows.

All colors were modified in value with additional white and Yellow Ochre.

PLAYING BOYS

Children at play is a subject dear to artists in every period of painting.

Engrossed in make-believe, children have something in common with the artist—imaginative power to conceive as real what is really fancy.

This illustrative painting is based on a composition of geometric planes in flat painting: the sunlit walls and roofs, the partition wall and the ground, as well as the figures. Depth is created by the vertical electric-line poles and the pole carrying the wash line.

The sunny color of the background is produced color and darkened in the boxes with Sienna and blue.

The forms underneath, suggesting shade, are of a violet hue warmed up with Ochre and Permanent Emerald Green.

The boy kneeling down beside the cart is dressed in Ultramarine Blue jeans and a rose-tan sweater.

The gray-brown cart is standing over a dark wet spot on the ground. The dark gray-green wheel of the cart with its characteristic ornamental shape serves as contrast to the rectangular forms.

The strangest manifestation of sunlight is found in the bright reds. The boy in the center is

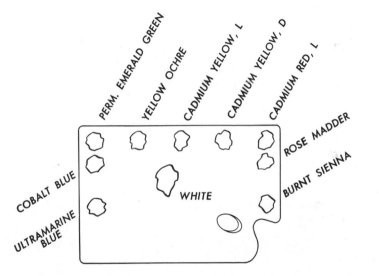

duced by small variations of warm colors and white: Yellow Ochre, Cadmium Yellow, light, and dark, and Cadmium Red.

The Cobalt Blue sky with its red clouds, the green roofs and the dark blue-black poles opposes the repeated color of the walls. The restful interval of the blue-white line of wash is painted across several of the houses.

At the top, the electric wires drawn across the entire picture have the same function.

Because I was purposely aiming at flat painting in every part of the picture, the figures are arranged as so many silhouettes.

Sand piles, cart, boxes and the play structure to the right are forms without perspective, permitting the idea of complete flatness to be carried out.

Sand piles are painted in Ochre-brown

dressed in a Cadmium Red shirt and the boy next to him in an orange-brown sweater. The sensation of warm sunlight is intensified by the contrasting, complementary blue in the jeans.

On the right-hand side the smallest of the boys with his gray-green sweater and Sienna colored pants links the bright colors with a blue-violet shadow on a distant wall.

Small incidental details like the center figure's hat and the sloping rib of the playhouse, both reaching above the partition wall, relate the foreground to the background without the help of perspective.

The feeling of depth and distance can be created in many ways. The magnificent formal perspectives of the Italian Renaissance are not necessarily better painting than the flat murals of the Orient.

MOUNTAIN VILLAGE, Italy

This motif was sketched a long time ago in a mountain village sunk into the dusk. The entire painting carries only flat values of warm, reddish browns, grays, and low-colored greens.

The main features of the scene are the geometric shapes, strengthened with jet-black shadows, of the background cliffs, the houses and the black-brown bridge in the lower center. A spot of blue-green water is under the bridge, dusty gray-green olive groves are seen here and there, and the Ultramarine Blue hues of the squares at the right edge, contrast in soft shades against the reds and browns.

Pink, blue-white and white-gray houses have Ochre and red roof-tiles, dark gray and black shadows.

The whole setting is contrasted against a glass-green evening sky.

The relative darkness of night can be effectively painted in cold as well as in warm colors.

A full color reproduction of this painting will be found in the color spread.

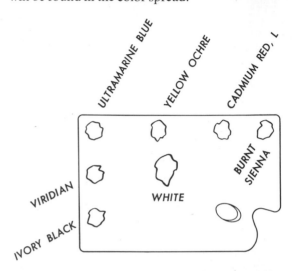

Chapter 8

Black Used as a Dominant

To demonstrate black as a dominant in a picture, a Viridian Green cup, a ball of black yarn, a white vase, and a lemon are arranged on an orange table set against a gray wall. Cadmium Red and blue, broken to a complementary gray with white, brings the picture into a harmony of three hues: green, orange and yellow; a triad harmonized against the black, white, and gray.

Burnt Sienna reflected into the black undersurface keeps the ball from floating over the shadowless table.

Motifs such as those illustrated in this painting—only a few simple objects in distinctive colors—are immensely useful in training the power of observation and are a good test for arranging color harmonies.

Black placed in a dominating position has been a sober and somewhat somber main feature

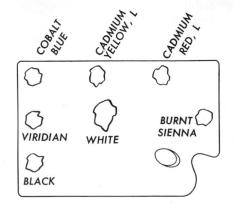

in creative painting from ancient times to our modern age.

Etruscan painters frequently let black play a dominating role in their wall paintings; a black horse, or simply a black framework gave strength and commanded immediate attention.

Later, black was given a significant role in portrait painting. In some painters' works a black background accentuates the light over the face, hands and details of white garments, ending in a monochrome of black and white. Conversely, the method of painting the features dark against a light background, in warm or cold colors, lends prominence to black garments, or sometimes only to black hair and piercing black eyes contrasted against a sallow face. These are but a few of the technical devices to bring forward the main object in portrait painting in depth.

Not to be overlooked is the storm landscape from the "wild-romantic" era. This was the period of landscapes with moody black stormy skies or black heaving seas. These well-worn dominants from long ago are still popular in contemporary painting.

The extensive use of black color is prevalent in much modern painting. There is nothing wrong with it, but there is when artists think that the black has a miraculous ability in itself to save a bad painting. Skeletonizing with black, for instance, to bring strength and additional values to a weak painting, is futile. Pictures that do not have enough chromatic power to begin with cannot be expected to receive additional color strength from a treatment with the light-absorbing black. Monochromatic painting in white, black, and gray, planned in advance, would be much more satisfactory and would have freshness and simplicity, instead of giving the impression of a repair job.

Black can be utilized to represent color in contrast with appropriate complementary hues in the general color scheme. Well-planned color schemes with black placed in contrast, to check and balance, will keep brightly colored parts from falling out or producing harsh, discordant areas in the painting.

Matisse, the master of color as well as its opposite, black, has made such factorial use of the black, but only to represent something conclusive, not as a shading color.

Modern art has quite a few masters of the black color: painters who use black freely and successfully to replace color in representing light. Matisse's painting of a black interior is a fine example of the possibility of such use of black.

Yellow road-signs with black lettering have made the effectiveness of the complementary contrast of black well-known to every motorist. Similar devices in modern art are by now almost formalized means of creating new sensations of form.

A completely formalized system of black used in painting was devised by the Swedish painter, Nils Kreuger. He covered a fairly light oil-color underpainting, which had very slight modeling, with dots of black ink placed far enough apart to permit the underlying color to play through between the dots. By skillful use of the dots and some lines he created light and form, modeling as he went along. The paintings have a luminous feeling of light. He applied his method to any motif with equal success—a sun-filled day or the moody Scandinavian summer night.

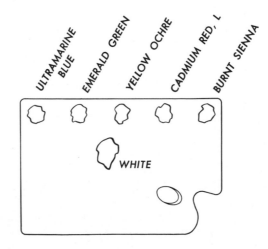

BLUE NIGHT, Scandinavia

This landscape, painted predominantly in blue colors, is divided into three sections showing progressive stages of work.

The first stage, at the left, shows the optic gray underpainting in white tempera over a light brown imprimatura.

The next stage, moving toward the center, shows the light transparent glaze of Ultramarine Blue over the tempera.

The actual painting, in the section at the right, starts with strong Ultramarine Blue over the sky and the water below. Reflections from the sky are scraped into the water, exposing the underpainting.

The wall, starting in the left foreground and receding into the background at the right, carries some red, gray, and green brush strokes to keep it forward. The dark blue shadow on the road in front of the wall is lighted with Yellow Ochre. The same light, coming from an unseen lighted house beyond the dark tree at the right, is thrown on the bushes beyond the road.

The foliage of the dark tree at the right is modeled in dull green; Burnt Sienna is reflected into the shadows.

TWO FARMS

The problem presented in this exercise is painting twilight over a farm landscape.

A watercolor I painted sometime ago in the farmlands of Dutchess county served as the subject for this oil painting.

Notice that the painting has depth and a feeling of perspective, although its elements are simple forms devoid of perspective and detail. There is a feeling of distance in the terrain between the stone fences even though these areas are painted in flat tones. The secret is painting cold and warm color in juxtaposition.

In order to avoid possible interference with the student's imagination and freedom of execution, only the set-up of the palette is given for this example.

The palette carries this limited range of color: Zinc White, Viridian Green, Ultramarine Blue, Yellow Ochre, Cadmium Yellow, both light, and deep, Cadmium Red, light, Alizarin Crimson, and Burnt Sienna. Medium #1 is the color thinner.

A full color reproduction of this painting will be found on the color spread.

I strongly recommend this type of subject to the beginner in landscape painting. A bird's-eye view is preferable to a ground view because it gives larger intervals of flat spaces. Paint a version empty of people or animals and with a minimum of objects, then do a second version of the same subject filled with figures in the manner of the Flemish painter, Brueghel the elder, or someone else of the same period. With your two paintings at hand for comparison, you will have a guide toward a positive understanding of the landscape seen as a composition.

A close study of the old masters, either in the originals or in color reproductions provides self-teaching material; inexpensive lessons that will be a great help in beginning landscape painting.

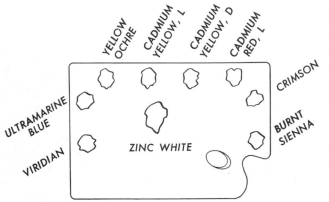

KNIFE PAINTING

Painting, or laying on colors, with a flexible palette knife or some sort of spatula can be very expressive if the limitations of the method are kept in mind. It is essentially a direct, one-stroke technique. Too much paddling with the tool will tire out the color. Loss of brilliance and after-darkening generally result when colors are over-worked.

The *alla prima,* wet-in-wet, approach and a clear idea from the start of what the finished painting will look like, instills freshness and daring into the work. Changes, or colors put down later as afterthoughts, have a tendency, in knife painting, to rob the picture of its all-important freshness or to cause its color to fall apart.

The subject should be selected wisely and carefully and then the impasto, or heavy color, put down swiftly and surely, and left alone.

The example shown illustrates the fundamental character of the impasto laid on straight over areas of scraped-down underlayers with the resulting vibrato. The materials used were black, white, half-white, Medium #2, and the trowel-shaped knife.

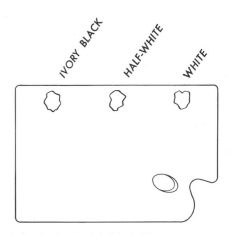

THE WHITE PAVILION

The classic serenity of this subject appealed to me from the moment I first saw it. Summer winds moved the clouds over the sky and shook the willows and poplars growing around the white pavilion. To me, the scene looked like a stage set for an old drama.

In spite of the strong movements of the heavy masses—the willows and the clouds—this picture retains the serene quality I first noticed in the subject. The white in the clouds, the white pavilion, and the whitewashed stone wall in front bring order and measured calm to the composition.

The blue sky—Cobalt with a touch of Viridian in the deepest places—was painted in short vertical strokes held together by the white in the clouds. The forms of the clouds were painted rose-gray, shaded pinkish-gray at the top and purple-gray lower down, with the white taking a dominant position.

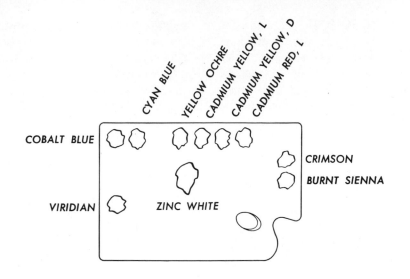

CYAN BLUE
YELLOW OCHRE
CADMIUM YELLOW, L
CADMIUM YELLOW, D
CADMIUM RED, L

COBALT BLUE

CRIMSON
BURNT SIENNA

VIRIDIAN   ZINC WHITE

The other two white areas are also in a commanding position—the pavilion standing on a foundation of brown-gray fieldstone masonry, and the stone wall. The gray-white wall was first undertoned in Ochre in even dots; then it was painted with Cadmium Red, white, and Cobalt Blue, letting the Ochre show through. The side away from the light was toned a pearly-gray. Soft shades in the same color values depicted the architectural features of the pavilion. The same colors were also used to make the bluer gray in the gravel walk. A blue shadow was drawn across the walk behind the black gate at the end of the white wall, and a darker red-blue shadow was added in the middle distance.

The only true red spot in the picture is a small building standing in this red-blue shadow. It is set in a patch of bushes and light green trees. Lighter yellow-green trees under the blue-gray mountain beyond cut off the vista.

Only a discreet use of ornamentation was necessary. I used such items as the pavilion banister, the detailed painting of the small spruce, and the ornamental iron gate for this purpose.

Values of strong yellow grass-green, broken by a few spots of gray ground, make up the entire foreground. The green grass was painted in short slanting strokes with mixtures of Viridian, white, and Cadmium Yellow, warmed up with variations of Yellow Ochre and

the deeper Cadmium Yellow.

Highlights on the brown and rose-gray dry grass are transitions to the other grays in the painting.

A group of trees treated as a unit fills the entire middle distance with light and dark masses of green.

Work on this unit began by undertoning the uppermost branches left of center and the light smaller tree to the right in a bright yellow which was promptly scraped. Then loose modeling of the other trees, except the poplars, was done in a warm gray-green made of Cyan Blue and Yellow Ochre which was also scraped down to a thin loose coating. Cobalt Blue added to this green made a cooler grayer shade which was used to shape the forms of the poplars, and was scraped down in the same manner to provide for looseness in transparency. Middle shadow tones made from mixtures of Cyan Blue, Ochre, and Cadmium Yellow, deep, were painted in only slight variations to loosely indicate the shadows over the dark trees. This was followed with darker mixtures of the same green, accented in depth with the blue and Ochre. Painting Sienna into this green gave still darker depths which modeled the trees into masses of foliage.

These forms were deliberately sharpened with Sienna and optic blue to depict branches and trunks bending in the wind. The gray underside of the willow leaves, turned up by the wind, showed the silvery sheen characteristic of willows. The gray for this sheen had more Cyan Blue and heavier white in it and was warmed with Ochre and a light touch of Crimson. It was mixed on the palette like the other mixtures, in a separate small pile. This system of preparing a few separate pre-mixed heaps of pre-tested color tones on the palette ready for use was employed by Cezanne and other great masters of color. The system is used on a larger scale by mural painters and scene painters.

Deep shadows in the gray-green poplars were painted in shades made of Viridian, dark blue, and Crimson, and were toned down by brushing Sienna into the shadow; these shadows set the poplars off against the sky and the lighter trees. The two lightest trees were finished in yellow-green mixed from Ochre and Viridian, with colder blue-green branches in front. Other yellow-greens show through the upper branches of the willow to the right. Blue optic light over branches in front of the pavilion, and small shadows in cold and warm grays under the trees were the final details put in to root the trees to the ground.

Beyond, reflections of light over a river and blue mountains are visible. At the right near the horizon the sky was touched with light pink.

Review

Let us briefly go over the main points to remember in painting a picture in oils; these points can serve as a check list to keep at hand as you paint:

1. Have a clear idea of what you plan to do and how you plan to achieve it. Think out the painting from beginning to end before you pick up a brush. This will come more and more naturally as you become more proficient.

2. Select your color scheme from the range of colors on the palette and try them out in sample painting.

3. Begin with loose, flat painting of the different elements in the motif. Leave detail until the end.

4. Lay in the underpainting.

5. Establish your dominant color scheme according to your original plan.

6. Add your supporting areas, always keeping control over the cools and warms and the general balance of the tonality.

7. If corrections of large areas are necessary, remember the erasure with tempera-white technique.

8. Add the necessary accents and the finishing details. Throughout the painting remember not to tire the color by overmixing, either on the palette or on the working surface.

9. Remember that each stage in painting the picture must look like something complete in itself.

The student who has mastered the techniques described in this book is well equipped to go on to Book 2.

Course

in Beginning

OIL PAINTING

Olle Nordmark

Introduction

The first book in this *Course in Beginning Oil Painting* dealt with materials and their proper use in various methods of painting. In this book I will explore a new approach to the understanding of color.

Color will become increasingly meaningful to the student as he learns to fully understand that this is the creative factor in painting.

The colorist's true strength lies in his ability to paint with relatively few pure colors; a painter who uses a profusion of different shades of colors is not a colorist.

The skillful colorist places contrasts in opposition and blends them to produce an effect of shimmering vibrato over his color scheme; he contrasts light with shadow. Although he paints with strong colors, he balances the whole picture in perfect harmony for the strong colors are quieted by passage tones.

These are a few of the principles the student must learn. Attempting to do coloristic painting without knowledge of coloristic principles will result in clashing colors.

The problems I shall deal with affect the professional painter and the student equally and are just as important to the one as to the other.

All problems, including the seemingly complicated ones, will be treated at the beginner's level but from the professional point of view. Throughout the series great stress is laid on the professional handling of materials and techniques so that real craftsmanship may be attained.

I hope that my efforts will bring you the joy of knowing how to paint. When your work begins to show the personal touch and the development of good taste I will have succeeded in putting you on the road to great satisfaction.

Olle Nordmark

Chapter 1

Elements of Coloristic Technique

To become a good colorist you must first of all understand *color realism,* by which I mean color as seen in Nature's ever-changing light, expressed in the terms of pigments on a palette.

Many people still believe that copying nature with photographic accuracy is "realism" because they do not understand what truly constitutes the reality of what they see. The landscape before us is enveloped by moving light that is constantly shifting its position, constantly producing new and different effects. The light is a hard or soft reality, as real as stone or water. Light alone can make the stone or the water real to us.

I will try to help you understand the color phenomena of light in Nature and how to put what you see on canvas. This will include the phenomena of *simultaneous contrast,* creating depth and distance by juxtaposition; the importance of painting in contrasts of cold and warm tones; building form; and how to see for yourself in order to paint the different component parts of color harmonies and color contrasts realistically. These are the "building materials" of color realism, the elements of coloristic painting.

In order to make proper use of these elements constant practice is essential. A student can delve into all the technical painting lore of the ages, study with many teachers and read many books, but his progress will be slow until he has acquired knowledge by practice. It is the only way to learn how to utilize painting materials and how to apply them most effectively.

Once you have grasped the technical side of painting it is time to study with the best teacher of all, Nature. It is my aim to teach you how to

learn from Nature. The examples and exercises in this course provide the kind of practice that will develop your talents and give you the confidence to paint on your own, directly from subjects of your own choosing.

Before you start a painting, aside from exercises, you should always take time to become familiar with your subject whatever it may be. Look it over and absorb your first impression. Do not stare at it intensely and do not try to memorize every detail. Instead, tilt your head back and half close your eyes. This way you will see the dominating features and the most striking components; you will get the essence of the

first impression. This definite *first impression* is exactly what you are going to paint. Hold on to it. You may stray once in a while, but always make an effort to get back to what you first saw.

If a particular color seems to remain with you the longest, that is your clue. Begin by setting in that color just as you saw it at the first moment. Build the rest of the color scheme around it, using hues that will not disturb the first color note.

Perhaps a certain light creates some effect that pleases you. Determine the colors and how they are grouped to give the effect you like. Place your colors, unmixed, on the proper part of your canvas *and leave them alone*. Work on the parts around them, always choosing colors that will not be out of harmony with your first tones. Then, later, the effect can be strengthened without having the color scheme fall apart.

You may find a certain form capturing your interest because it somehow dominates the scene. Then by all means let it dominate in your painting.

Sometimes an insignificant design will appeal to your imagination and become the key to the whole picture. The pattern of a large tractor tire or a rabbit spoor in the snow could serve equally well as the theme of a painting. Any such idea, however trivial it seems at the moment, should be recorded in your pocket sketchbook. It may turn out to be a jewel of an idea, more satisfying than any found by deliberate search.

Before moving ahead to actual painting instruction, I would like to make a few points clear:

Point one. To master painting you must learn to draw with brushes. The ability to draw with the brush is vital, especially in figure and portrait painting where a likeness must be retained.

Point two. Before you actually begin painting be sure you are ready to paint. You should be familiar with your subject. All your painting implements should be prepared.

Point three. The total tonality of a picture is often established by the first brush strokes. The vitality of a forceful and brilliant beginning will be carried throughout the whole painting.

Hesitant, colorless beginnings usually end up in bleak monotony.

Point four. Brighter, cleaner color schemes are obtained by observing some simple rule of color sequence in painting. In oil painting the warm colors are usually painted first; the cooler shades are laid on top of the warmer ones.

Point five. This is of great importance and must be kept in mind throughout the painting. Each successive development of the picture, however sketchy, should have the appearance of something complete in itself. If each stage is carried out with this in mind the picture will hold its tonality at later stages and it will be easier to keep the work under control as it progresses.

Chapter 2

Two More Colors Added to the Palette

In Book 1 the palette is described in detail. Beginning with this book the color range of the palette is widened with two additional colors: *Venetian Red* and *Ivory Black*.

After experience with the first color range, toned to the spectrum scale of color, the beginner will find many surprises in the new combinations of colors made possible by the two additional hues.

Venetian Red mixed with white yields delicate cool values of silvery quality, valuable in painting the nude. Employed with discretion in landscape painting and laid on pure into greens,

are the colorings of rainstorms, and thunderstorm skies. These grays can be further deepened with Crimson and Ultramarine, or blackened with Viridian and Crimson.

The Venetian Red is "friendly" with all the other colors on the palette. In harmonies of warm hues it should broaden the general effect in a manner quieting to every part of the picture. Because of its very strong color saturation a little goes a long way.

Venetian Red is a warm color, therefore it is placed on the right side of the palette, under the Burnt Sienna. Ivory Black is a cold color

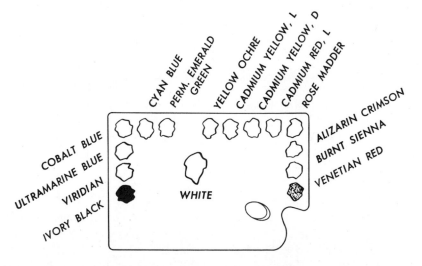

shadows, and red objects, Venetian Red gives warmth to other colors but with less garishness than shades of the brighter reds.

Mixed with a blue, this warm, intensive red produces characteristic heavy grays that can be broken into colder or warmer tones. In simultaneous contrasts with bright yellows, purples, violet, and so forth, the effect will be less saccharine than with stronger reds.

The massive heavy grays of the Venetian Red-Cobalt mixture, controlled by adding white,

and belongs on the left side of the palette, below the Viridian Green.

Now we have Burnt Sienna and Venetian Red set out on the right side, and Viridian Green and Ivory Black on the left. Thus the palette, with the Yellow Ochre in the middle and the white below the ochre, is divided into *cold* on the left and *warm* on the right side.

Black and white are contrasting colors. Neutral black is neither blue, green, nor violet, though it can be broken into any of these three because of its cool value. But it cannot be made to look like a red, orange, or a yellow. This gives it a distinctive quality as a complementary color.

Beginners generally think that black is most useful in the mixing of dark, deep tones. Actually, the real function of black is in painting airy, light nuances of half-tone strength, within combinations with white.

Solid areas of pure black, in contrast with strong pure colors, act as balancing and checking complementaries of dark and light values. But if *added* to bright hues black weakens them down to a grayish sameness at best. The dull, grimy values that result from such mixtures will deaden the tonality in much the same way as painting with leftovers from a dirty palette.

When painted in transparency, black can be of great value in tonal painting, in transparent painting of an evening sky, or as an almost invisible glaze over a brightly conceived painting in numerous gradations of color.

Renoir used black as a unifying thin glaze over some of his paintings. He studied the old masters' methods of handling black glazes and used such glazes effectively to produce the silvery values found in his paintings.

The Impressionists banished black from their palettes altogether. Van Gogh resolutely put it back on his and found the right way to use it, namely in light tones and as a contrast, and also in black and white contrast. Even his black contour served in a contrasting capacity. To mute the loud color-concert of complementary colors in strong hues, which he painted against each other, he skillfully made the most of black in one way or another, staking out the field for modern art.

Modern masters, like Matisse and others, have developed and refined the use of black as a real *color* factor and thus incorporated the black color into their paintings. The phenomenon of black participating in active competition with the clearest, brightest colors on the palette can be seen in modern paintings where the black could not, in some instances, be removed from the color scheme without upsetting the chromatic balance of the whole picture.

Black, to another modern French artist, Braque, had an entirely different meaning. He combined the color with earthy browns, dull greens, blues, violets and grays. In much of his work a golden yellow, alone, functions in the capacity of a contrasting counterpart. The careful attention given to cool and warm in spacing out the values is common to both Matisse and Braque; intervals of gray play an important role and the black acts as a normal basic color.

In some of Braque's paintings the black is broadened into flat planes of shadow and heavy, wide contours designed to bring out form in somber patterns of light and dark. In some of his pictures, sharply defined differences in the value of the black effects are carried to all parts of the canvas by deep browns, grays, and a very active yellow. In others, rhythmic, horizontally laid out forms move along over predella-like paintings. (The predella is a narrow, long painting placed under an altar painting and resting on the altar itself. This is a format of early easel painting.)

Braque, early in his youth, learned how to use marble and wood-grainers' tools. The "grainers" were craftsmen who imitated marbles and woods, substituting painting for the expensive genuine material. The markings from the wood-grainer's "oak comb" are frequently seen in Braque's oil paintings. This tool is well-known to the author, who also grew up in the old shop tradition of the carriage painters and the grainers' craft.

With their bold new approach, considered revolutionary at the time, the early masters of modern art have helped us understand the laws of color and form.

NOVEMBER DAY

This painting demonstrates the effectiveness of the Venetian Red we have added to the palette.

The tree group in the background to the left, standing against a cold green sky, is illuminated in pale autumn light of white, Yellow Ochre and Rose Madder. Standing further forward is another group in dark blue. A blue-purple shadow reaches out over the Ochre ground. Shadows drawn over the ground indicate the distance of the background.

A greenish-yellow light, and darker blue shadows set off the Venetian Red color of the buildings, establishing the beginning of the general color scheme.

Venetian Red, with Ultramarine Blue brushed in and lightened with white, is painted over the wall to the left. The resulting purple shade is strengthened with Crimson in the deeper shadow. Pale Ochre light over the open door is divided by a dark blue shadow.

The dark interior was first sketched in with Sienna, then given depth and drawing with Cyan Blue and Crimson. Subdued light over boxes in blue-green, mixed from Ochre and Cyan Blue, makes the necessary contrast against the red of the exterior.

The cold, purple-gray shadow dividing the roof is a followup of the purple-blue and Crimson under the eaves. The warm light over the door changes to a warm gray where it continues over the roof.

A brilliant spot of color from the afternoon light is seen on the foreground. This is painted

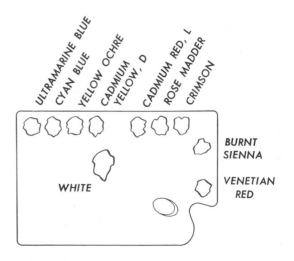

in Cadmium Yellow with white.

Cadmium Yellow, deep, is mixed with Cadmium Red to bring out the strong color effect on the strip of wall over the door-opening and the right hand door. Concentration of brightness like this, in the center of a painting, tends to keep order and clarity in compositions where many sharply defined shadows are painted in cold and warm contrast.

The same red carried over to the building on the right, slightly toned down with Sienna, makes a lighter, milder opposite to the bluish-white trimming and the blue-green in the window panes.

The wallboards are outlined and drawn in Sienna. This is done by using a flat brush held between the index finger and thumb and run flat against a beveled straightedge. The bevel is turned down and one end of the straightedge is lifted slightly to keep it from rubbing against the wet surface.

Warm rose-gray and purple shadows color the bare trees behind the buildings, in sharp contrast to the white trunk of the birch in front. Pale blue shadow, yellow-white light, and black markings bring this strongly lighted tree out into the extreme foreground.

Turn to the color spread for the reproduction of this painting in full color.

Chapter 3

Color Saturation

Saturated, unbroken colors are pure colors that have not been mixed on the palette. They must be painted boldly and unhesitatingly. Pure colors can be laid in directly on the canvas in several ways. The results, though achieved differently, have the same thing in common—a vibrant, colorful freshness.

The direct approach helps the beginner by taking the fright and bewilderment out of painting. Facing a myriad of nuances of colors and values often sets up panic in the novice, but the simplicity of the coloristic technique gives him confidence. For instance, suppose you need a dark, purplish shadow-spot in the foliage of a tree. Pick up a blob of Rose Madder or Crimson on one corner of a flat bristle brush, and on the other corner a blob of Viridian Green. Wiggle them into the greens of the tree. This way you will immediately say in one operation what cannot be said with the same freshness in long, painstaking brushwork. Thus, two complementary colors, set in unmixed, work like magic in appropriate relation with other colors—especially where strong sunlight strikes some particular color.

Of course there are many other ways of getting the same effects. But this method is a good way to start learning how to achieve rich texture and a fresh, lively color surface without the overworked look of what the Norwegian modernist, Edward Munch, so aptly characterized as "the nail-and-twig-painter school."

If you lay your colors down either in a single tone or in pairs, one on top of the other, or side by side, without any deliberate attempt to mix them, you will get loosely blended colors arranged in a vivid array of values. Your canvas will look fresh and clear.

The truth of this can be seen in the outdoor paintings of Van Gogh. The tonality in some of his earlier works, which were painted in somber color schemes, has sunk into almost complete darkness. At a certain point he changed from this murky palette to a free and direct technique, using the saturated colors of the Spectrum Palette. By outlining the color areas with a contour he was able to control the tonality, although he painted fast, and without restraint. The contour, black or in color, remains in some of his paintings; in others it has disappeared entirely or merged with the adjacent forms.

He succeeded in imbuing his pictures with the colors and forms of life, with the light itself. They have depth although they are completely flat paintings. Juxtaposition of the tones, and brush strokes that give the direction in space, provide every pictorial value. He was able to depict form, solidity, airiness, depth and distance —all without academic painting "in the round."

The techniques evolved by Van Gogh should serve to clarify the meaning of direct painting in unmixed, saturated colors.

Chapter 4

Color Control

To guide the student a step further toward the understanding of the uncompromising complementary colors, which are a law unto themselves, let us visualize the following theoretical exercise:

The over-all purple-blue tonality of a painting is to be moderated in tone and chromatic strength by complementary contrasts.

Painted into the purple-blue, distinctly separated strokes or dots of orange-red will cause the purple-blue to move toward violet-blue, the orange-red bringing out the complementary blue. The still closer color, red, would incline it toward blue and blue-green. As another example, a dominating tonality of purple-red, suffering from the use of too strong reds, oranges, and violets, can be tamed; the offending colors can be brought to their proper values by painting warm dark greens in small areas of the composition. The colors will be modified but their intensity will remain intact.

Georges Seurat, the French painter, who was Van Gogh's extreme opposite in temperament and manner of work, developed a scientific system of color control. He made small on-the-spot studies which were not much more than quick notations of light, color, and locale. These impressionistic sketches, with all their freshness and spontaneity, he later enlarged to heroic proportions in his studio. Time and again he went back to the spot where he had made the original sketch to compare it with the progress of the painting in his studio.

Seurat prepared himself for painting a picture by working out the whole composition in preliminary studies. With these, and a clear idea of the finished painting in his head, he could work freely on his canvas in the studio. After dark he continued painting by artificial light, sitting on a high stool before his huge canvas which was lighted by a ramp of gaslights like a theatrical backdrop. He would set down minute dots of pure color, dot by dot, side by side, without blending—a method he had worked out mathematically. He had formulated this method in precise systems: the grouping of the figures, a system of pictorial structure, the division of the pure colors and tonal gradation. He also used linear forms as linear harmonies and contrasts—half circles and curves, verticals, horizontals, and diagonals—to reinforce the pictorial structure. These systems became more and more complex as he proceeded from picture to picture. The precision of the color is fascinating in its unbelievably accurate building of the light and shadow components of the picture.

The painting method exemplified by Seurat's work is known as Pointillism. It is a more systematic plan than any other form of Divisionistic Painting, sometimes known as Neoimpressionism. It is defined as a method of painting in which colors are separated into their component hues, and these hues, in pure color, are laid side by side on the canvas in order to blend together in the eye of the observer. The effect of the blending is seen as a third color with a higher degree of vibration and luminosity. This is what we mean by *simultaneous contrast*.

Seurat knew exactly how many blue dots should be painted on the canvas and the number of yellow dots needed between them to produce a particular green.

By intensifying this green with separate dots of blue and a number of red dots, a true shadow-color appeared in the green.

Working methodically in this way, he kept the entire canvas under complete control.

Seurat's scientific system of painting has brought us much valuable information and added to our knowledge and understanding of the laws of light and color.

Control of composition and design, by the

spacing of the unifying moderating colors, must always be in full accord with the undertoning. Exaggeration of contrast should be avoided in order to keep a proper balance between light and color.

Abstract tones of white, black and, by intermixture, the resulting gray are also by the nature of their nuance harmonizing elements in painting. If these are centered in, or grouped around a grating color, the discord is reduced.

Chapter 5

Beginning the Painting

Make a guiding sketch with as few lines as possible. It can be transferred or drawn lightly on the painting surface. Have your palette and brushes arranged. Now you are ready to start painting.

Begin by filling in the allotted space for each color in flat painting using strong color as pure as it comes from the palette. Do not weaken the colors and your initiative toward a strong, colorful beginning by unnecessary diluting with white. Only colors with a high degree of saturation, such as Ultramarine Blue and Cyan Blue, always require the addition of white; however, Rose Madder, Crimson and Venetian Red usually benefit by a small amount of white; and a little white added to Yellow Ochre gives it brilliance.

Scrape the brushed-out colors down with the palette knife to give them looseness without loss of chromatic strength. Colors that turn out to be entirely wrong should be removed by scraping, not by wiping with a rag. A new shade should be put into the scraped spot with a minimum of rubbing. Aimless, undecided brush-rubbing will deaden any beginning. Adjustments of colors and values are made at later stages.

Do the painting all at one sitting (*alla prima*) and allow it to dry in full light, but not in sunlight. Oil colors that dry in the dark will turn yellow, especially in the stale air of a closed room or closet.

When painting *alla prima*, wet in wet, make sure you have enough clean brushes on hand so you will not get dirty mixtures on your brush. Picking up a lighter color on a brush that has been used for darker paint, or vice-versa, will deaden the colors and stifle every effort at brilliance; gray half-lights and half-shadows will introduce themselves everywhere in the color scheme. Use the brush rinsing jar containing turpentine for quick cleaning.

At the conclusion of Book 1 a check list was provided which covered briefly the main points to remember when painting a picture in oils. It is repeated here since it applies to any painting and to any stage of proficiency.

1. Have a clear idea of what you plan to do and how you plan to achieve it. Think out the painting from beginning to end before you pick up a brush. This will come more and more naturally as you become more proficient.

2. Select your color scheme from the range of colors on the palette and try them out in sample painting.

3. Begin with loose, flat painting of the different elements in the motif. Leave detail until the end.

4. Lay in the underpainting.

5. Establish your dominant color scheme according to your original plan.

6. Add your supporting areas, always keeping control over the cools and warms and the general balance of the tonality.

7. If corrections of large areas are necessary, remember the erasure with tempera-white technique.

8. Add the necessary accents and the finishing details. Throughout the painting remember not to tire the color by overmixing, either on the palette or on the working surface.

9. Remember that each stage in painting the picture must look like something complete in itself.

Picture 1. Monochrome

Chapter 6

Painting a Tree

Close-up painting of individual trees of the leafy variety can be very bewildering. As the beginner looks at the seemingly endless detail in the leafy masses he wonders where to begin! Here is a clear, easy, illustrated procedure that will be reassuring.

Intricate objects, like trees, are begun in monochrome painting, using only light and shadow in two values. This method will teach more and teach it faster than the tedious painting and overpainting of the trial-and-error method. The monochrome is valuable as a teaching example and will also serve as an underpainting, or base, for the overpainting to follow. Drawing the object with a round brush in monochrome in two values will get the job under way.

Picture 1, showing the tree in monochrome, will be helpful in studying the distribution of light and shade over the mass of leaves. It shows how three greens divide the big mass into leafy forms. This monochrome is painted in Cobalt Blue mixed with some Flake White and thinned with turpentine to watercolor consistency.

Picture 2 shows the first stage in the overpainting, or the first stage of the actual painting. Begin this by mixing three shades of green: a light tone, a middle tone, and the shadow. The palette is limited to half-white (Zinc and Flake White), Cobalt Blue, Cyan Blue, Permanent Emerald Green, Cadmium Yellow, light, Yellow Ochre and Burnt Sienna. For thinning, Medium #1 is used.

Start by mixing the color for the light tone —white, Permanent Emerald Green and Cadmium Yellow, light. Make a small heap of this on the palette. Now mix Permanent Emerald Green with Cyan Blue (which has been pre-mixed with a small part of white). Warm the tone with Yellow Ochre. This is the second heap

of color on your palette; it is the value of the middle tone, also called a half-light.

The third heap of color, the darkest shade of the greens representing the shadow, is a still darker mixture of Permanent Emerald Green. Add Cyan Blue, Ochre, and a minute amount of Sienna to make it the darkest, warmest value in the composition.

Picture 2

Medium gray for the trunk and branches is made by mixing white and Cobalt Blue; variegated shading in the light and shadow is done with Sienna and Ochre. This gray and the middle tone of green are used for the narrow patch of grass and sand under the tree.

Look at Picture 1, the monochrome in blue. The lightest of the greens is painted in the places marked "light." Then the shadows are set into the allotted spaces to bring out the tree's leafy shape and volumes.

Next, the blue underpainting of the branches and the tree trunk must be worked over to clarify the structural part of the tree.

Then, in a leafy fashion, or in leaf-shapes if the student wants to paint actual forms, the middle tone is painted over the light areas, leaving enough of the light color uncovered to

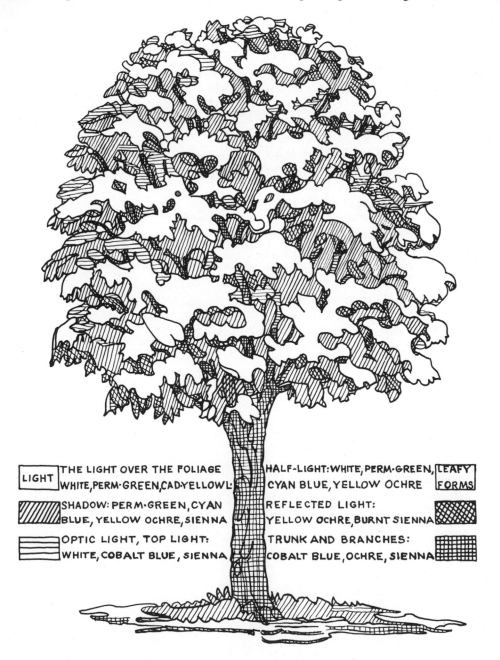

LIGHT — THE LIGHT OVER THE FOLIAGE WHITE, PERM·GREEN, CAD·YELLOWL	HALF-LIGHT: WHITE, PERM·GREEN, CYAN BLUE, YELLOW OCHRE — LEAFY FORMS
SHADOW: PERM·GREEN, CYAN BLUE, YELLOW OCHRE, SIENNA	REFLECTED LIGHT: YELLOW OCHRE, BURNT SIENNA
OPTIC LIGHT, TOP LIGHT: WHITE, COBALT BLUE, SIENNA	TRUNK AND BRANCHES: COBALT BLUE, OCHRE, SIENNA

Picture 3. Graphic Analysis of Tree Painting

support the design. Spots of reflected light are painted into the shadow, using Yellow Ochre in the lighter areas and adding Burnt Sienna to the Ochre in the darker places.

Full modeling in light and shadow is now complete. At this point look at the painting from a distance to check the chiaroscuro and the structural precision and relationship between leaves, branches and the trunk. Make the necessary corrections before adding the finishing touches.

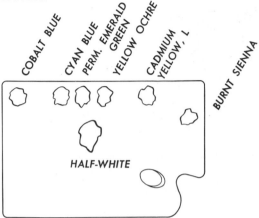

After the corrections are made, optic light in blue-gray (blue and white with a touch of Sienna) is added on the upper surface of the left side-branches. Remember that this is atmospheric light, so keep it light and airy in feeling. Use the complementary opposite, Cadmium Yellow, to light up transparent leaves on the outer edges of the foliage at the upper right and lower left.

Strengthen the shadow on the inside branches, and set in the occasional light spots created by openings in the foliage. Check the trunk for light and color.

Once you correctly understand the building up of the masses, in form and form-building color, you will be able to paint any tree without much difficulty. The actual brush work should be done in a completely personal manner. Each painter should try to find his own style.

OLD PINE

This fine old pine, standing on sloping ground, had tight and evenly grown branches, distributing light and shadows in even rows of green. The green local color, Viridian broken to a warm shade with Ochre, shows only a few variations.

Toward the top of the tree, the color changes to a gray-blue. Lower down it is green. This green is made warmer by adding Yellow Ochre variegated with Cadmium Yellow.

Ultramarine Blue is used to make the dark green in the shadows even darker and further accents of depth are painted into it with Crimson where needed. Still further down, this colorful shadow is enriched by reflections of the color from the ground below, painted in slightly orange-colored browns of Ochre and Sienna.

In certain reddish lights, like the sunset glow, Venetian Red or the brighter Cadmium Red, sparingly set into the shadows, is very effec-

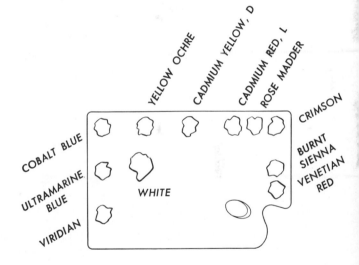

tive without heightening the color scheme to gaudiness.

Around the upper, outer fringes of the green, transparent Cadmium Yellow, deep, helps to model the green masses in soft silhouette.

Within the tree under the dark green shadows, branches are painted Ultramarine Blue. The deepest places are shaded down with Cadmium Red and Crimson. This purple-black is effective in any spot where special depth is needed, for example, against light or the sky.

In the full light, the warm grays of the trunk, branches, and the stones are variations of Cobalt Blue and Venetian Red, with drawing in Burnt Sienna.

The colder optic light from above is a light blue made of Cobalt Blue and Rose Madder with some Venetian Red, to give the typical blue-gray of the optic light seen on surfaces turned upward.

The local green is used again for the bushes and grass. Where needed, it is made brighter and warmer with the Cadmium Yellow, deep, and Ochre.

Only round brushes were used for this painting. The work was simplified by using the same kind of brushes for every stage of the work. The #2 painting medium was the only color thinner used.

AGAINST THE LIGHT

The noon light of a September day floods this scene. Two dark groups of trees are silhouetted in sharp contrast to a sycamore branch in the foreground. The branch is painted in bright transparency.

Because of the massive shadows, strong, deep colors are necessary when painting objects seen against the light, as in this picture. The only guiding lines needed are indications of form drawn lightly with a medium hard pencil around each area of color.

This direct painting was done in pure saturated color. The color was mixed as little as possible. The #2 medium was very sparingly used as a thinner. One large and a few smaller round brushes were employed.

Zinc White and Titanium White, mixed half-and-half, controlled the values in the lighter mixtures. Only a few tones were loosely mixed on the palette. Dark colors in particular will be lost in a hopeless black before they even reach the canvas, if they are too energetically brushed and scrubbed on the palette. Should colors turn too dark after they are on the canvas, the best remedy is to take the palette knife and scrape the area down to a light thin coat; trying to rub the color off with a rag will only make things worse. Do this exercise as follows:

Begin with the sky. Paint light pink, white, Ochre, and some Cadmium Red in the cloud formation. Around the clouds lay in Cobalt Blue in semi-opaque color, controlled with white and a very small amount of Viridian to give the sky-blue a light sheen of greenish blue.

Next, paint the meadow in a rose-gray. The light over the dry grass interspersed with goldenrod, is drawn in short brush strokes with Cadmium Yellow, light, and deep. Foreground goldenrod should be painted as brilliantly as possible and forcefully accented in the lower right corner by setting in a Sienna shadow. To the left, paint strong, vertical brush strokes of Ochre and Sienna to reinforce the foreground colors and to form a base for the brighter shades above.

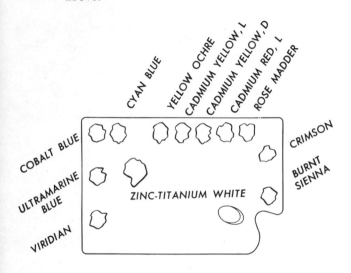

Two dark groups of trees stand out against the sky. By painting the darkest tree group in the center middle-distance first, the dark volume becomes a practical guide to the evaluation of color tonality and the chiaroscuro of all the other objects.

Do the first modeling of the trees and bushes in Ultramarine Blue and Ochre, which will produce a gray-green. Scrape this down to a thin transparency. This scraped-down gray-green serves as a unifying undertone and is seen here and there in the foliage.

Mix Cyan Blue with a little white and use it in conjunction with Viridian and Ochre to model individual branches on the right side of the group. Further in, a darker mixture of the same green is broken into with Ochre and Sienna deepened with Rose Madder. Round off the branches in the light by highlighting and modeling, partly in warm gray-green and partly in gray-blue green, with an occasional sharp glint of light. Draw branches and trunks in Sienna and Crimson to add the extra dark values to the shadow needed to complete the forms.

In the distance, beyond the meadow, use the same colors again to paint the dark shadow over the smaller tree groups. The only difference is that the coloring needs to be made colder. Make it blue-green and purple-black.

Behind this distant group, use Cobalt Blue and Viridian, in a lighter blue-green, and paint into it with Viridian and Crimson, to shape the forms of the silhouetted trees. Lighter trees in Ochre mixed with Viridian stand in the light reflected from the meadow. They enliven the color scheme with their warm tones in opposition to the cooler blue-green shades.

Closer to the ground in the shadow, strong strokes of Sienna will provide the necessary warmer depth.

One-third of the subject is dominated by the sycamore branch with strong sunlit brightness seeping through the transparent leaves, counterbalancing the dark volumes behind. Use yellow-green, in light shades of Cadium Yellow, light, and Viridian for the underpainting, adding colder gray, blue, and green on top. Still darker leaves, branches, and shadows are painted in more detailed coolness with Cyan Blue, white and Viridian, accenting them in depth with spots of Ochre and Sienna. Cadmium Yellow, deep, and Ochre, for the reflections from below on the larger leaves nearer the foreground, will bring the main foliage forward. Viridian and Sienna, in drawing around the hanging branch, will cut it free from the background shadow.

Paint a blue-green shadow under the big branch and draw the twigs and branches in Sienna, adding blue-gray spots of optic light. This, together with openings in the foliage done in sky-blue, will set the sycamore foliage apart from the darker colors.

Finally, put a dark blue shadow under the center group to cut it loose from the yellow grass in front, and then your painting is complete.

Chapter 7

Painting in Contrasting Colors

Here is the very foundation of modern painting. Brilliant harmonies in strong colors are distributed over the whole canvas without modeling or shading. The flat forms are painted area by area, guided by a light charcoal drawing. The surplus charcoal dust must be slapped off lightly with a rag, before painting begins, to insure clear coloring. Strong color tones, creating harsh contrast, are modified by painting the contrasting complementary colors into them. The pure, true complementaries should be avoided; instead, select from the *near* complementaries, not the direct opposites.

In Book 1 the complementary effect and its practical application in painting is fully explained: the color triangle explains the complementary contrasts; important color-mixing exercises are given. These exercises will help the beginner understand the effect of complementary contrasts.

Effective building up of form and space in the painting is not only the result of painted modifications of the color surface such as shading, crosshatching, texture, or superimposed ornamentation; the spatial life evoked finds its beginning in the different juxtapositions of the color.

The discreet introduction of a cool tone, selected from the opposing hues, divides the tonality into distinct cool and warm areas that will assert their harmonizing influence over every part of the painting. Exaggerated chromatic strength means loss of light. Loss of color-strength occurs in overemphasized light. Hard light throws the finer transition tones into monotony because dark shadows and dark backgrounds are needed to bring out the brilliance. However, in a simple, dark, and strikingly distinct color scheme with darkness predominant, a glaringly hard light, painted in broad, flat patches of color designed to transmit the feeling of light penetrating darkness, can create interesting effects. Forest interiors, parks and architecture are only a few of the traditional subjects where this special light is the main factor.

Contrasts in color can be held down to a minimum to let the values play a dominating role, harmonized in cold and warm. The brightness of light itself creates brilliant patches, such as spots and streamers cascading down the deep forest interior or in the interior of a cathedral. Both have the same shadowy gloom in common. The light piercing the darkness seems to have the brightness of spectrum color. The beautiful and interesting spectacle of light filtered through stained glass windows is a wonder of color in action. The light seems to change each object it brings into view.

The forest interior is a good example of a dark, contrasting background for the red, rose, and yellow colors of the light. The deep blue, deep green, and violet shadows, with orange and Burnt Sienna reflected into them, form the dark contrasts against which the bursts of light are painted.

Colors having close similarities of value and strength can sometimes be painted in to create a pleasing effect on the surrounding hues. The addition of a few well-planned forms, somewhat ornamental and smaller than the forms of light and shadow, will enhance the harmony. Simplified ornamental forms are often seen as supporting elements in modern painting.

SUNLIT FRONT YARD

This painting is presented in five steps to show its gradual development from start to finish. Sharp contrasts between light and shadow are the main features. The range of the palette is restricted to a few colors. The color scheme is planned to depict warm sunlight.

Deep, warm shadows and equally warm light are contrasted with a few soft values in cooler tones—the sky, the house to the left, and the flagstone walk. Intermediary cool shades of color are used in the shadows. Warm colors painted in strong, warm values are held together by introducing areas of pure white. In this case I made use of the white trim on the house and the white picket fence, a "natural" in this type of subject. The preliminaries for the painting were color notations made from observation of light and shadow, and loosely drawn pencil sketches of anything that could not be committed to memory alone.

The palette consists of the following colors: Viridian, Ultramarine Blue, Permanent Emerald Green, Yellow Ochre, light, Cadmium Yellow, light, Cadmium Yellow, deep, Cadmium Red, light, Alizarin Crimson, Burnt Sienna and Zinc White. Painting Medium #1 should be used as a thinner.

Step 1. Shapes and shadows are drawn on the canvas with a hard, pointed charcoal stick. The outline of each form is drawn in a single, clean line. If you find the subject too complicated, make the drawing on tracing paper, or some other thin, strong paper; then rub the back of the drawing with a soft pencil and transfer it to the canvas by running an empty ball point pen or a hard pencil along the drawn lines.

Begin by painting the sky. Ultramarine Blue and white are mixed to a light shade of blue, thinned sparingly, and painted over the sky area in a thin straight coat. A bright, which is a flat short bristle brush, is used for this work.

Now paint the undertone for the grass. This is light green mixed from white, Permanent Emerald Green, Yellow Ochre, and a touch of Cadmium Yellow, light. It is painted out in the same manner as the sky, but with more looseness in the vertical brush strokes. Underpainting with this half-covering green provides a cool base for the final painting of the grass and takes an active part in the color texture of the surface. For smooth-flowing color, thinning necessary.

The strips of green between the pickets of the fence can be drawn with a flat, narrow brush. The grass growing between the flagstones is outlined with a smaller round brush. Use the same green, made cooler with a small portion of Viridian, as the foundation color for the light over the trees and the flower beds. The light and the shadow on the two chimneys are put in with

white, Sienna, and Ochre. The same warm shade is used for drawing the tree trunks.

Step 2. Two important color contrasts are painted next to secure an orderly development of the color scheme: the blue roof to the left and its direct opposite, the rust-red roof to the right. These two colors are of equal importance to both the cool and warm colors surrounding them. The blue roof is Ultramarine Blue mixed with white and grayed a little with Sienna. The color of the red roof is made of Cadmium Red and Cadmium Yellow, deep, subdued with Yellow Ochre.

On the left side of the house, the wall is in cool shadow. This is painted in white-mixed Ultramarine Blue, grayed a little with Cadmium Red. The end wall in the sunlight is a pinkish

white made of white-mixed Cadmium Red. The window shades are the same color toned down with blue. The brown-red door is painted in transparent Sienna and Cadmium Yellow, deep.

The small trees standing behind the fence are underpainted thinly in a warm green mixed from Viridian, white, and Cadmium Yellow, light, slightly lowered in value with Ochre.

The house wall to the right is swept by strong light, which is partly a reflected light influenced by the light over the ground. This twin problem is solved by painting the wall in a warm color that is both yellow and red: Burnt Sienna lightened in tone with white, and Cadmium Yellow, deep. Later, against the dark green shadows in the last stages of the work, the yellow-red wall becomes a simultaneous contrast, and will be self-luminous, although no effort has been made to paint light.

Accents of darkness are set in the windows with Viridian and Crimson. Stone steps and the walk are painted in a stone-gray made of blue, white, Sienna, and a touch of Crimson.

Clarifying lines in Burnt Sienna are run on the edges of the roofs. A simple method for painting straight even lines is to use a number four bright and draw along a straightedge raised at an angle. The color must be thinned to flow smoothly and evenly from the brush. The brush handle should be held lightly between the thumb and index fingers.

Step 3. At this point the shadow forms in the trees, the hedge, and the two flower beds are outlined in light charcoal drawing. Then they are painted in shadow green, which is a mixture of Viridian and Yellow Ochre, cooled a little with white-mixed Ultramarine Blue.

Step 4. Light yellow-green leaves are added next, over the warm underpainting of the small trees. Emerald Green, white, and Cadmium Yellow, light, lend a spring-green lightness and a bright contrast to the painting in general.

The long shadows reaching across the lawn are outlined in charcoal and painted in a deep green of Yellow Ochre mixed with Viridian. Do not mix white with the Viridian in this case, since here we want full saturation of the green. The same mixture is used to paint the dark shadows of the hedge and flower beds. The grass from the fence to the house is darkened to indicate an area in the shade. The shadows in the foliage are again thinly painted with the shadow green described in Step 3, but with slightly more white-mixed blue added to give the color a blue-gray atmospheric tone. Then paint the iron railing, and the blue shadows over the steps and the stone walk.

Step 5. At this stage the top of the sky is given more depth by adding enough Viridian to the original sky-blue to make an airy blue-green.

The heavier atmosphere below is painted with warm rose-pink, and white and Crimson warmed up with Yellow Ochre. Where the two colors meet they are thinly shaded together to form a lighter semi-covering middle tone.

The light and shadow-tones on the chimneys are finished at this time. The color of the blue roof is deepened. The red roof is enlivened by light and dark shingles. Beyond this roof the blue-gray misty form of a distant tree is set in.

Short brush strokes of Permanent Emerald Green, lightened with Cadmium Yellow, deep, and some Ochre, are employed in modeling the round tree top. The lighter undertone is left here and there to activate the modeling. Brush strokes of a deeper shadow color—Viridian, Ultramarine Blue, and Cadmium Yellow, light—and a few more strokes of a still deeper shade made by adding Crimson, round out the flat shadow. These two shades of dark green are set into the shadow of the two remaining trees, with small variations of tone in Ochre or Cadmium Yellow, deep, occasionally deepened with blue and Viridian.

The light on the two trees standing in front is modeled in Viridian and Cadmium Yellow,

deep, with the deeper, stronger yellow moving forward. Setting off the color in heavy blobs, using small brushes, will help to control the light over the branches. Strong, warm sunlight over the trees to the right is depicted in a light shade of Crimson and Cadmium Yellow, deep, with white. This sets up the sense of movement and shimmer called *vibrato*.

Branches drawn in Sienna and blue, and cold blue spots of light on the trunks, shaded lighter as we move downward, lend structural strength to the trees. Strong strokes from a wider brush bring the light over the lawn into sharp contrast with the long shadows. The green of the grass is a loose mixture of Permanent Emerald Green, Yellow Ochre, and Cadmium Yellow, light.

Trunk and branches of the larger tree to the left are finished with blue-gray shadows and warm light made of white, Ochre, and Sienna.

Light, the deeper shadows in drawing, and Ochre-Sienna reflected light, give finality to the hedge and flower beds.

Purple peonies in Crimson, red, and blue, contrast against the yellow wall. Lighter, warmer light brings the flagstone walk into color balance with the general light. The shadows across the walk are strengthened with optic blue-red. The curtains, the flower-pot, the shadows in the windows, the reflected light over the left side of the door, in Sienna and Cadmium Yellow, deep, and the round brass door knob are the final details of the yellow house. White trimming and the white picket fence finish the picture.

Turn to the color spread for full color reproductions of Step 4 and Step 5.

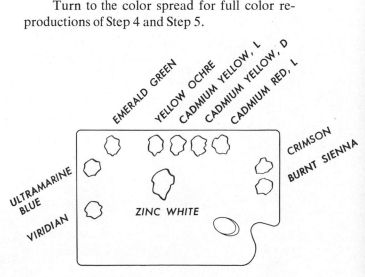

REFLECTED COLOR.

The experienced painter sees a rich reflected light in the shadows and he can control the richer color scheme. If you learn to see and understand reflected light, color-enrichment of every part of your painting will result.

It is not necessary to use a great many variations of color in reflected light. The following experiment demonstrates the principle. It is done with two cards, each one painted in opposing colors. One card is placed in strong light and the other card is placed in the shadow. Let the light reflect from the first card into the shadow of the second and you will immediately see what is meant by reflected light or color.

Use an inexpensive set of showcard colors, corresponding to the palette, to do this experiment. They are more practical than oil colors for this purpose, as showcard colors dry immediately, ready for the test.

Here is how the experiment works (*see illustration*). Paint one-half of a card in rose lightened a little with white, the other half in a clear red. A second card is painted all over with a bright yellow. Reflect the yellow over the first card held in shadow and study the changes taking place in the two reds. Reverse the effect by placing the yellow card in shadow, and reflect the reds into the yellow. Two other cards, one painted blue-green and one painted red, will show an entirely different change of tone.

Variations with brighter and weaker colors, darker and lighter colors, should be tried out in the same way. Simple experiments such as these do not take much time or effort and they make the principle of reflected light easy to understand.

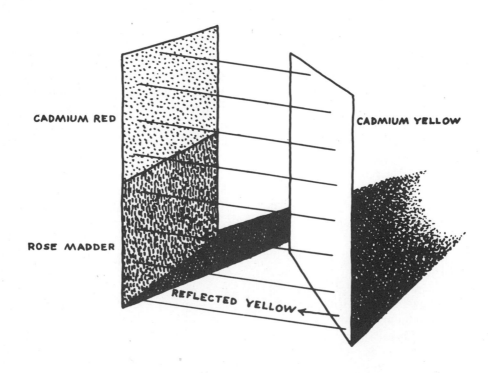

CADMIUM RED

CADMIUM YELLOW

ROSE MADDER

REFLECTED YELLOW

BAR

This painting shows how reflected light can be effectively handled with a severely limited palette. Seen through a half open door, a lanky figure is standing at a bar. The cold light from the outside competes with the electric light to create the gray quality of the color scheme.

Only three colors, Cadmium Red, light, Yellow Ochre, and Ivory Black, were used, with half-white in a value-controlling capacity. In conjunction with the white, black produced blue-gray; by adding Ochre a green-brown, a black-brown, and a red-brown was produced. By moderating, harmonizing each tone against the other, a great variety of color tonalities come naturally from this very restricted palette.

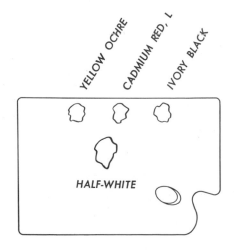

The internationally known Swedish painter, Anders Zorn, used this limited range of colors in a manner bordering on virtuosity, the only difference being that his Vermillion is exchanged for Cadmium Red, light, on our palette. If I remember correctly, he used both Zinc and Cremnitz White in his paintings.

This painting is done in cold and warm, with tonal contrast in cold light and warm shadows. Only slight attention is paid to local colors. To contrast with the ochre-colored shirt there is pink in the face and arms, a purple tone, made of black, white, and red, in the hair, and warm light-purple on the neck and arms.

The gray-brown bar and the floor in the cooler light from outside, make the dark background for the figure. The bottles on the shelves reflect the cold light against the Ochre and red walls behind.

Summing up the possibilities of this restricted palette, the silvery light and the warm shadows, when free from muddy accidental mixtures, are effective in the extreme. In figure painting, painting of the nude body, for interiors or for outdoor scenes this unusual tonal range can meet the most demanding pictorial realism. It is especially suitable for subjects with a sharp difference between light and shadow, where shadows in saturated browns and highlights in whites are possible.

Medium #1 is well adapted to this method of painting.

Chapter 8

The Dominating Color

Dominating does not necessarily mean that one color, or one form, alone, takes command of the whole picture. The dominant should give strength and support to the surrounding subordinate values.

The first colors painted on generally determine the color scheme of a picture. With this in mind, the painter should use color samples to pre-test and organize his color masses. He will arrive at a satisfactory color scheme more quickly and avoid messy corrections.

In *Coloristic* painting, where strong emphasis is laid upon color as the major component, the problem of the color scheme grows with the complexity of the subject undertaken. Here, more than ever, the painter must be well prepared before painting actually begins.

Accomplished colorists do not leave anything to chance. The color scheme is well thought out and tried out in advance. Painted samples, in accordance with the colors on his palette, are made up by the artist for the purpose of arranging them into harmonies on his canvas. By moving them into different positions, creating new contrasts, new effects, he can get a preview of his color scheme.

These samples are usually done on the white painting-paper that will be described later. Highly saturated colors, like Ultramarine Blue, Cyan Blue, Rose Madder, Crimson, and Venetian Red, are premixed with a small addition of Cremnitz White or Flake White for direct use on this type of paper. The tones are pressed out with the palette knife, so a thinner is seldom needed.

Gouache colors, or showcard colors, corresponding with the palette, can be used for making larger samples of cut-out forms and broad effects to be studied as elements of the painting.

When a satisfactory arrangement of the color tones, represented by the samples, has been found it may still be necessary to make small adjustments here and there. A sample may be repainted, or a fresh attempt made on a new piece of paper. One sample will often turn out to be the outstanding shade around which the other color samples can be arranged into a harmonious whole.

This kind of experimentation with samples is true coloristic technique and is used by every trade that has anything to do with colors anywhere. To resort to the hit-and-miss method of painting and repainting on the actual final canvas in order to learn how to establish a color harmony is a waste of time and materials. It is outright foolishness to expect something to turn up accidentally. Preliminary work with the samples will insure freshness, the clarity of a unified color scheme, and speed of performance in the actual painting. These are the features of a good painting—the unified whole rather than divided unorganized detail.

When you have found a suitable tonality, it is time to practice actual painting of a subject. These first trial paintings should be done on inexpensive materials such as the painting paper mentioned before. This paper is embossed to imitate canvas and comes a dozen sheets to a book. The sheets are 12″ x 16″, but cut them in half, to 8″ x 12″. This is the most practical size for beginning oil painting. The Bee Paper Company, Inc., 1–9 Joralemon Street, Brooklyn 1, New York, manufactures white and a slightly darker oil painting paper that I can recommend. Most art stores carry it or some other brand of painting paper.

Stick the paper to a piece of plywood or to a drawing board with bits of scotch tape, keeping the embossed side up. Draw only the main forms of your picture, lightly, with a charcoal stick. Now you are ready to begin practice painting in the color scheme you have decided on.

Many trials will have to be made with the samples and in actual painting before the beginner can expect to have a clear understanding of the complementary colors in contrasts and harmonies. Here the trial-and-error method is used to the utmost. If the first try does not come up to expectations, number it #1 and begin the second, but avoid slipping into the same mistakes again. Each trial painting of the same subject should be made as speedily as possible, using flat masses of color. With this method, a fresh approach is possible in each one.

I know of one outstanding colorist who made as many as twenty-nine paintings from the same model on canvas approximately 28″ x 39″, before he found what he wanted.

Experiments are beneficial to the imagination; for example, half-covering casein-white-priming done crisscross or streaky on brown paper will give the effect of grained wood. Experiments in varying the undertoning and experiments in the painting itself should go hand in hand.

The author's earliest experience of painting with oil colors began by painting on a homemade painting surface. Ordinary thick, strong, brown wrapping paper was cut into suitable sizes and thumbtacked to a drawing board. Whiting mixed with glue-size to a paintable thickness was applied in two thin coats. The first coat stretched the paper taut and after it had dried out completely the second coat was applied. If hard, strong, white paper is used, the first coat should be thinned slightly with water and applied as glue-size, followed by the second white coat as before. Commercial showcard white is too weak for the priming, but now we have ready-made casein white which is excellent for this type of painting ground.

Fearless painting, in quantities, on inexpensive surfaces, without concern about spoiling canvas, will not only lead to painting discoveries but to the evaluation of one's talent. Real concentration and effort spent on each tryout is of immense practical value in understanding color.

Each trial painting should be numbered. After ten or twelve such research paintings have been done, lay them on the floor in sequence. Seeing them all together is both revealing and rewarding. Select the one you consider best.

When the canvas, drawing, palette, and the selected trial painting are ready, painting can begin. The paintings, if not too large, should be painted wet-in-wet at one sitting. If this is not possible they should be allowed to dry thoroughly between each stage. Painting on two, or even several pictures will give the first one time to dry while you work on another. Remember that wet oil paintings must be left to dry in full daylight (not in the sun) to prevent yellowing of the colors. If they are turned against the wall, the same yellowing effect will occur, due to darkness and the pocket of dead air. Use thinners sparingly. In *alla prima* painting only painting Medium #1 is needed for adjustments of the color thickness.

Be careful not to make a half-tone by rubbing two full tones together. The half-tone, or half-light as it is called in painting of the nude body, is a transition and is usually referred to as a passage tone. It should be mixed separately. In painting light over the body, the passage tone runs as a neutral middle shade of gray between the light and the shadow. Half-tones that are used as stepping stones from one contrast to the other are subdued shades of either or both colors. All half-tones serve as color tranquilizers in the painting.

Distinctiveness of hue is the mark of real craftsmanship in coloristic painting. No individual color is allowed to fall out of the general scheme; all are made to work together. Each is a participant in the entire harmony.

Passage tones can prevent strong colors from becoming too prominent. A third color, reduced in brightness and set between two powerful colors, serves even better to establish balance; centered in a group of strong colors, such a device provides a resting place for the eyes. Sometimes a gray made from two near-complementaries and placed between them will accomplish the same purpose. One color helps another —checks and balances it. For example, in a painting with yellow, red, and blue, a cool green centered in the painting helps to harmonize the yellow and the blue and quiets the red. The tonal placement of the yellow and the blue preserves the equal strength of all the colors in every part of the painting.

By experimenting with the color samples in combinations of different contrasts, the student will have the system of the complementary colors clearly laid out before him. Arranging them in opposites, in dark-light values, will produce simultaneous contrast, which gives the illusion of a third hue.

Moving color samples around is the simplest way to avoid wrong color combinations and find out what will "click."

The behavior of light and color in direct opposition should always be kept in mind. Strong colors have a tendency to dim the light in a picture, while strong light weakens the color tonality. Strong hues in harmonious relationship keep the chromatic power in balance.

If you observe the sunlight over a landscape by looking at a group of trees you will see that sunlight makes the trees look almost colorless. A passing cloud, screening out the light for a moment, brings the full color back again. The sunlight gives the impression of strong *light,* not of a decidedly strong *color.* Rose or pink does not change to look like orange, nor does blue-green change to yellow-green. Only the direct relationship of colors in contrast will do that. In cold light, warm colors seem to take on additional warmth; in warm light they seem to grow cooler. This is an example of the power of contrast.

When I began to study art, one of my teachers said to me: "Nature always expresses herself in terms of light and dark, never in white and black. Even the whitest thing in nature, the snow, is expressed in the light-producing spectrum colors; the darkest night is expressed in the deepest blues, greens and purples."

SKI HILL

This painting is done by laying on and spreading the colors with a flexible palette knife.

Trees, skiers, the two crows, and the lumberyard are the only details painted with brushes. Use two small flat sable-hair brushes and a lettering brush.

A small thumbnail sketch is all you need when doing a painting of this type. It is not necessary to draw your sketch on the canvas.

The distant snow-covered hills against the lower sky along the horizon are painted in a light gray made of white, Cobalt Blue, and Cadmium Red. This mixture makes a luminous cold gray. Since it is repeated in several places, make enough to last until the painting is finished.

The two roads curving around the hill are laid in with a pinkish gray warmed up with Yellow Ochre. Blue-gray is scraped into this, with the traffic tracks in a darker gray. At the top of the road on the right-hand side, pale green fills the space with light.

The ski-run is painted over in an off-white yellow, which will serve as a foundation for the pure white to follow.

The premixed light gray is used again, for undertoning the trees and around the rocks and the two roads.

Venetian Red and white, mixed, is used for all the houses. Variations in cold and warm tones are made by adding more or less white to the red. Blue and blue-green wiped over the red creates the frosty color seen on the stone buildings standing in the field higher up.

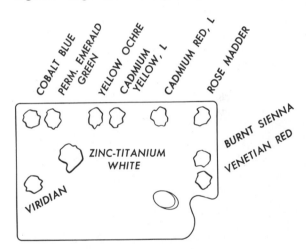

The gable of the house standing in the lower left corner is darkened with blue. The eaves and the door, drawn in the same color, are made to balance the black rock.

Two houses in orange-red contrast effectively with the cooler tones. Each snow-covered roof is pinkish white, blending with the snow in the far distance. Thus, the distant brick-colored buildings have the lighter, coolest colors; those nearer the foreground, the warmest.

Orange-Sienna brightens the lumberyard at the right. The gable behind the yard is made frosty-cold by using Cobalt Blue and white in uneven knife strokes.

Complementary black, mixed from Viridian and Rose Madder and a warmer black made with Sienna and Cobalt Blue are the two blacks used in the trunks and branches of the trees and for drawing the rock formations.

The two crows are drawn with additional blue added to make them blue-black.

Light over the trees, painted in small blobs of frosty, pure white, separates them from the light-gray background. Pure white shapes the snowdrifts on top of the rocks, along the sidewalks, and along the lumberyard.

The color scheme of the traffic-worn roads is knit together by a blue-gray sidewalk and trees along the left road, with pink-white and Permanent Emerald Green on the opposite side and pink and blue over the lumber.

The boys are dressed in bright red woolen caps. Sweaters and pants are pink, red, blue, and blue-green, with some in darker shades of Ochre and Sienna. The skis, poles, and sleds are orange Sienna. The small white stripes on the cap and sweater of the skier rounding the curve, are painted with the lettering brush and the small, flat sable-hair brushes.

Tracks in the snow are drawn in pure white.

The sky is laid in last. It is undertoned in a light green, made by adding white to Permanent Emerald Green. Into this undertone a light white-pink, made from Cadmium Red, light, is spread with the knife in brush-like strokes. Here and there Permanent Emerald Green is drawn into the rosy-pink cloud formations at the left, toning down the pink to a pink-gray.

At the right-hand side, light blue put in over the pink and green, darkened at the top, produces the cold color of snow clouds. Use the same blue to darken the left side of the horizon. From the center over to the right, the color changes to pinkish gray.

Zinc-Titanium White and minute parts of Flake White added to the Rose Madder and Crimson control the color values. Medium #2 is the diluent, or thinner of the colors.

Many variations of shades in gray, resulting from the pink and the green, turn up under the painting knife. It is, of course, impossible to describe them all correctly.

The basic mixtures in each of my paintings are simply leads for students, to teach them to see for themselves. They should learn to experiment and work directly from nature. Whether realist or modernist, the only colors we see and paint are those seen in nature, or color memories from nature's own arrangements of hues.

MOONLIGHT

The essential color of moonlight can be painted successfully by using only five colors. Ultramarine Blue and Burnt Sienna, varied with Viridian, Cadmium Yellow, light, and the softer Yellow Ochre are the chief colors of both light and shadow.

If you keep your palette always set up in the same order, you can paint by moonlight, or at dusk, without having too much trouble finding your way around the palette. Keep in mind that mixing two complementaries will produce black. This will do much to simplify painting by moonlight. The author has painted winter moonlights outdoors in seventeen degrees and colder!

When painting outdoors in winter a few drops of castor oil in the turpentine will keep

the colors workable. However, the colors will run when you bring the painting into the warm studio, so lay it flat to dry out.

One of the main pitfalls in painting moonlight scenes is the total blackout of dark objects against the light of the moon. Look at the example above and you will understand what I mean. Notice that the house is not entirely plain black in silhouette. If so, it would fall out of the atmospheric feeling of the painting seen as a whole. To avoid this, begin with the light and middle tones, then move to the shadowy darks.

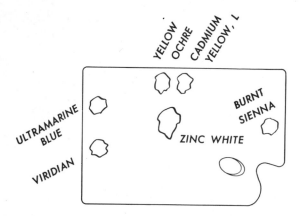

This painting is done as follows: Beginning with the sky, the dark openings between the clouds are painted in Ultramarine Blue and white (Ultramarine Blue is always premixed with some Zinc White). To the left, these openings are made warmer and darker with Viridian and Ochre. Further away, in the upper left corner, they are made still darker by using blue darkened with Burnt Sienna. The light over the clouds is pink-gray—a mixture of Sienna and white painted wet-in-wet into the blue haze and shaded bluer at the top. Closer to the moon, Ochre and light Cadmium Yellow gild the edges of the nearby clouds. The same Ochre gilding follows the edge of a cloud bank slanting upward to the left. Under this line, the cloud shadows are deepened in pink-gray. Closer to the house they are warmed with more Sienna. At the horizon they are bluer.

Trees and bushes on the opposite shoreline are loosely modeled with Viridian painted into dark blue.

The moonlight to the right side of the house illuminates the trees in the distance across the water. This is painted in shades of Viridian

warmed with Ochre.

The ripples on the water reflect the moonlight in silver and gold. The water is simply painted in values of the sky and the clouds and in the same atmospheric tonality. Later, after drying, the streamers of light on the water can be repainted to strengthen the illumination.

The boat and the bridge planking are gray-blue, slightly warm. The shadows are in a still warmer gray, made by adding Sienna. The lighter and bluer grays of the boat are reflected in the water. To the right the water is painted dark blue and the reflections from the moon are painted in bright yellow.

The dark silhouette of the house is a simple gray of Ultramarine Blue and Sienna softened with white. To the right, the adjoining building is blue-gray and the roof is in a half-light of more blue, with shadows in brush strokes of brown over Viridian. The knoll in the foreground is of the same quality as the color of the house, with cold blue reflected light in the deeper shadows of the uneven ground.

Grass-covered ridges in the foreground are highlighted with soft shades of cooler and warmer gray-brown. Dark shadows in Viridian and Burnt Sienna are used for modeling the tufts of grass, bushes, and folds in the terrain. The top leaves of the bushes are silver-gray.

An old oak and a willow, standing behind and beside the house, have a warm dark undertoning of Viridian and Ochre. Over this tone, the leafy masses are modeled in blue-green; the shadows are a dark loosely painted mass of Viridian, Ultramarine Blue and Burnt Sienna. Tree trunks, branches and leaves silhouetted against the haze around the moon are drawn with a round brush in a warm black made from blue and Sienna. Foreground bushes are finished in the same technique and coloring.

The moon is painted in strong Cadmium Yellow, light, in thick color, sharply accented against the haze around it. The haze is painted in a mild tone of Ochre and Cadmium Yellow, light. This simultaneous contrast leaves a soft glow over the sky.

A feeling of warmth is given to the inside of the house by the lamplight shining through the small window panes. The orange tone of the lamplight is a mixture of Sienna and Cadmium Yellow, light.

Chapter 9

Picture Control

Here are a few simple devices that you will find helpful for checking the color and values in your paintings.

Using a mirror is probably one of the oldest methods—the reverse image will reveal faults quickly and accurately. In the drawing stage and later in various other stages a painting should be checked and re-checked with a mirror to detect errors. A common hand mirror with a perfect glass is fine for this purpose. In a studio, a large wall mirror is usually used for checking large paintings. Such common flaws as wrong proportions and "leaning" are hard to discern with the naked eye. The mirror image shows them clearly.

Another device is the black mirror, attributed to the French painter Claude Lorrain (1600–1682). In the old days it was considered an almost indispensable part of the landscape painter's equipment. I am including this simple device because of its value to the beginner. A ready-made piece of black mirror glass can be bought for very little at any art store. Or you can make one for yourself from a piece of glass of mirror-glass quality. Give the back a couple of coats of automobile "touch-up" black, and trim the edges with gummed black-paper strips. I have seen some old black mirrors with a movable arm clamped to the easel. During outdoor painting, the easel and the mirror were arranged in such a way that the picture values could be compared with the image in the black mirror from time to time as the painting progressed. The useful features of this simple device are the instant valuation of the relationship between light and shadow (the chiaroscuro) and, to a certain extent, the proportion of broad masses and the color values. I do not recommend it as an all-round help for color as well as for chiaroscuro, because the finer tonal variations in color are drowned in the black. Nevertheless, you will find a black mirror very helpful. Methods and tools do not lose their value or become obsolete merely because they were used in a bygone era. Old studio and paint-shop tradition laid the groundwork for much of what we know about painting today.

Many painters use a reducing glass to get a concentrated all-over view of a painting. Some use a camera with a ground glass. Scene painters often employ neutral pure-blue glass or a piece of the blue gelatine used in stage lights to examine warm yellow, orange, orange-red and particularly light-yellow highlights. By looking through the blue, a complementary opposite, the chroma or the strength of the yellows and yellow-reds, can be tested for brightness. Weak spots are without glow and show a red-brown blurring, a sign of insufficient chroma. This is another demonstration of practical control of the complementary colors.

The time-honored way of looking the subject over is simply to frame the subject by looking under the elbow of the raised arm, or by cupping the hands. Looking through an opening in a card, cut to the proportions of the canvas, is even better.

These are the devices most commonly used for finding spots that need correction. Defects will show up in very much the same way by looking at a painting in candlelight, at dawn, or at dusk.

Even moving the eyes from a picture that has become familiar and looking at it again with a fresh eye will give you new impressions and a truer evaluation of light and color.

WHITE HOUSE IN A PARK

This painting, from a sketch I made in Scandinavia, does not have the gray of a rainy sky. It has the misty gray of diffused light, which is the light that Cezanne called "the light of a clear gray day." The shadowlessness of such a day reveals much that is fundamental in painting and the effect on colors should be clearly understood. Under an overcast sky the local colors of each object come to the fore. With sunlight absent, color is influenced only by contrasts created by the actual colors of each object, called *local colors*.

To gain effective tonality (the all-over color-tone of the painting) the local colors are set against each other in contrasts without mak-

ing use of the strong pure complementaries. Garish color should never be allowed to take a lead in this type of picture.

Passages in pearl-grays in the sky, optic light, gravel walks, and so forth, act as mild intermediary contrasts between intervals of grass, hedges, and other areas in stronger local colors.

A light undertone was painted over the entire surface, using a mixture of white, Ochre, and a small part of Rose Madder. This was left to dry.

The subject was outlined in pencil, lightly drawn on the dry undertoning, using just enough lines to space out the different color areas.

Colors for the trees in the foreground were mixed in two piles on the palette and tested for tone and value on a piece of white paper. Permanent Emerald Green, used as the basic green, was premixed with a little white, and for the light tones broken with Cadmium Yellow, light; for the shadow tones, Viridian and a small portion of Cyan Blue, also premixed with white, were added. White in the top greens made the color cooler; and Yellow Ochre below made the greens warmer. Rose-gray and Sienna shadows edged with blue harmonized with the trunks and branches and contrasted mildly with the foliage and the brighter green of the grass.

The background hedge, in the same basic green, was darkened by painting into the shadow with Crimson and Sienna. In this way, the lawn retained its fresh yellow-green strength, but was kept from falling out of the color scheme.

Foreground ridges of grass and lighter color patches were brightened with yellow and variegated with bluer green. In two places darker spots showing the bare ground were indicated as rectangular violet-blue shadows—under the tree to the right, and less pronounced, close to the bottom of the painting where the grass has a warmer green value. Sienna shadows in still stronger values indicate the slight unevenness of the ground under the larger tree, the trees in front and further back.

Before work began on the background, the all-important passage—the bluish-gray gravel path—had to be painted between the green intervals. This gray also had to harmonize in a mild manner with the yellow-green, therefore the path was made lighter and warmer toward the distance.

Cream-colored light and blue shadow, together with the light-colored red roof opposed by the blue-greens in the window, centered the house as a bright, colorful spot in the picture.

Orderly sequence of painting the different elements in the subject must be sensed by the artist. Here the sky, and the darkest objects, the poplars, were left until last.

The two silhouetted poplars immediately show whether the greens are in right relationship in the shadows. This is important because greens cover the largest area in the painting and therefore must be painted before the smaller, darker objects. The two poplars were first modeled in a light blue allowed to show around the edges. Next they were deepened with Ultramarine Blue, Viridian, and given additional depth by modeling in Rose Madder. This produced an effect of blue-purple and blue-green as seen against the warm greens of the foreground trees.

The darker bushes below, done in blue-green with warm Sienna shades, have silvery-gray highlights. A deep purple between the tree trunks marks the deepest depth of darkness inside the tree group.

Light shades of Cobalt Blue with white, alternating with Cadmium Red with white, were painted out over the sky in half-covering criss-cross brush strokes. By letting the yellow undertone come through in the half-transparency, the blue and red shades were activated into a pinkish gray of a pearl-gray quality, bluer at the top of the sky. Sky color, in a dark value, made the mist over the trees in the far distance. Two angular spots in bright yellow oppose a shadow in violet at the opposite end of the lawn. An orange contour under the roof and yellow-lit edges on the branches of the greens draw the harmonies of the color closer together.

For a painting of this kind only a few colors are necessary when correctly selected, and the scantiest of contrasts are needed to harmonize color tone against color tone.

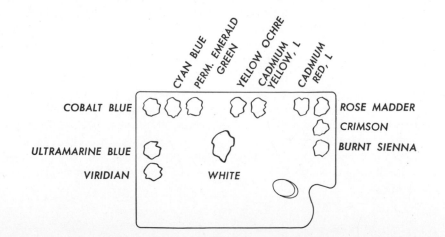

LUMBERYARD

A rainsoaked maple standing between the sidewalk and the street is centered in this picture. A fence running along the sidewalk and a lumberyard provide the pictorial background.

The half-light of a rainy day is the main painting problem.

Intervals of wet cement walks in blue-gray, and the gray flagstones leaning against the gray fence are the contrasting cool colors. These intervals are spaced out between the strips of green grass, providing a counterpoint of cold gray to the mass of warm color in the green leaves.

Inside the yard, stacks of lumber in light yellow are seen against lanes of wet ground painted ochrish white and rose-gray. A strong note of blue-black is found in the pile of steel pipes on the ground to the right. Alongside the pipes, and in a few spots on the opposite side, the light green grass is a helpful note of color in support of the light rosy color on the open yard.

The more complicated painting of the tree must be organized beforehand, as explained previously in *Painting A Tree*. First, three shades of green are made up on the palette. A general light green is made of Permanent Emerald Green mixed with white and the two yellows,

Cadmium and Ochre. Tryouts are made on a piece of painting paper. These will show that the next value should be a darker, deeper green with Cyan Blue and more Ochre added. We now have the light green and a medium dark green. A still deeper green to represent the shadow is made by adding more Cyan Blue.

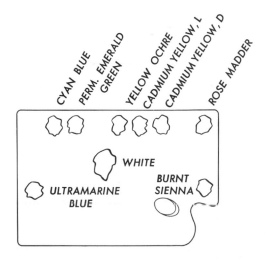

The tree is begun by painting the leafy masses in a modeling fashion throughout, using the light green. By dividing the leaves into regular branches, using the next darker green, the whole tree emerges. Into these two darker greens, reflected light from below is painted in Ochre and Cadmium Yellow, deep, making a fairly sharp contrast in orange-yellow. In some places, still deeper shadows build form with the help of branches drawn in Burnt Sienna. Surfaces turned upward have the typical cold gray-blue optic light, painted to represent shining wet leaves.

Black, mixed from Burnt Sienna and Ultramarine Blue, is used to paint the wet bark of the trunk and branches, with a lighter gray tone closer to the ground. The same warm black is used in clarifying drawing along grass and walks, in the mirror effect of the tree trunk in a puddle of water, and in the light in the foreground.

Half way between the trunk and the right side, following the slanting rain, the colors from the top down are painted in a lighter shade, accented by patches of light Cadmium Yellow, to indicate sunlight breaking through.

Long streaks of rain finish the picture. Indicate the sharp, light, illuminating streams of rain by using the edge of the palette knife drawn lengthwise with blue-white scraped up on the edge of the knife. The same effect can be gotten by using the palette knife to scratch lines into the surface while it is wet. This is easily accomplished if one is painting over a hard white priming.

NAVAJO PASTORAL

Traveling inside the Navajo reservation years ago, enroute to Chinle near Canyon de Chelly, I saw this subject right after a heavy snowfall. The scene was painted from crayon sketches made on the spot, and detailed notes for the palette, color scheme and light.

A blowing snowstorm is seen hanging like a white sheet over the nearby hills. Far distant, dark gray storm clouds set off the pure white snow scene with hardly a variation in the white other than blue-gray in the shadows close to objects on the ground.

The storm-sky was first thinly painted with a warm gray made from Ultramarine Blue and Venetian Red. Using the same colors again in a deeper, darker mixture with very little white, depth was created with Cobalt Blue for the lighter, bluer notes, such as the top portion and the angular blowing clouds. Basic shades of the red and blue set up simultaneous contrast in the murky dark—the two complementaries creating cloud movement. These near-pure complementaries produce the airy grays of the sky. In their darkest values they never become too heavy, and they will retain their color values even when painted in sharp contrasts.

The snow-covered hills, to the right, are a blue shade of the gray made by adding Cobalt Blue. Detail—lines in the rocks, dots representing pinons (pines) and juniper trees—are drawn in Ivory Black, with some Ochre dabbed on.

On the left, close to the edge of the painting, is a single snow-covered pine. Further in, is a log hogan, the sheepherder's home. Details of the wall logs were loosely sketched in Sienna, then completed in cold black and white on the snowy side of the hogan and in black and Sienna on the darker side.

Sitting on the pile of logs is the Indian sheepherder, covered with a blanket in greenish shades of Cobalt Blue and Ochre. His face is a

weather-beaten, deep dark brown. The tawny color of the hat, and the tawny moccasins inside a round shadow of dark blue complete the figure.

Approximately the same colors were repeated in the logs, with the same blue-gray shadows.

A row of snow covered, cut-down pinons stands across the entire foreground. Immediately below, a row of sheep covered with wet snow gnaw the sparse grass. The Sienna, black, and gray of the pinons is repeated in painting the sheep.

Yellow grass has a hint of cooler shadow under the sheep. The grass and the blanket together comprise the strongest warm color in the whole picture.

Black smoke, mingling with the sky, comes from a stove pipe in a black area of soot on top of the hogan.

In the Navajo Pastoral I used gray-white passages and darker intervals, well-known devices of the old French and Flemish painters, especially in the 15th Century. During my long experience in designing for the stage, I found these devices extremely helpful for creating the illusion of distance in landscapes. The same principle applied in picture painting brings calm and order to crowded scenes.

The old masters, with the help of such pictorial devices, have given us many examples of paintings of classical calm. These are a well of knowledge available to any student. The principle of passages and intervals should be studied by looking at the works of masters in museums and in art books. Observations should be put down in a notebook. A wealth of useful ideas can thus be obtained with little effort and expense.

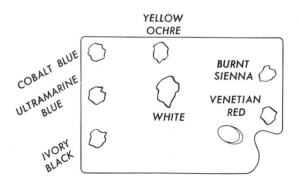

Chapter 10

The Still Life

The still life has always maintained its importance as subject matter in painting. For generations paintings of still life and flowers, in one form or another, have been popular as decorative wall paintings.

Beginning with a simple vase or a bowl of fruit, the still life was developed and added to until it became an independent work of art. Still life paintings have, in some periods, acquired documentary importance as mirrors of contemporary social life: paintings overburdened and overflowing with pictorial representations of the good life of the burghers. These have been able to compete, both in size and fascinating pomposity, with the best of the historical battle paintings.

A grand vista—a landscape flanked on one side by architectural forms while the other side was partly cut off by a decorative drapery—was a favorite background for the more elaborate still life paintings.

Household goods, from silver plate and glass to kitchen utensils, were heaped on a table together with fruits, flowers and all kinds of game and fowl. These incredible paintings were developed in perfect, realistic detail with minute exactness in every part, even to a fly on the peeled orange and drops of water ready to roll off the leaves of a bouquet of flowers. The drop of water nearest the foreground often had a window reflection in it, as in a convex mirror!

Developed into magnificent show pieces, they still hold the attention of an amazed museum public. They are looked upon today as wonderful documents testifying to the technical skill and knowledge of painting by early masters in many countries, who executed them in every known painting technique from fresco to oil painting.

The French painter, Jean Batiste Simeon Chardin (1699–1779), taught us the artistic value of kitchen utensils. In his paintings, pots and pans in the scullery are wonders of beauty. His still life and paintings of home life—at the breakfast table, the kitchen chores—are among the finest documents of human life we have; paintings filled with charm and beauty speaking to us in a still, small voice.

To this day the contemporary Italian painter, Morandi, does not stray very far from his bottles and shells, covered with magic dust and light. Morandi's paintings of what we would label as junk evoke a deep feeling of restful detachment.

SETTING UP AND PAINTING THE STILL LIFE.

The still life provides one of the best subjects for painting instruction. A few items on a table are all that is necessary for the study of every problem found in painting.

There is an old axiom that says the artist who is capable of painting a still life or a flower piece will have no difficulties with other subjects. It is still true, and the still life or flower piece remains a basic method for developing painting skill.

The work can be done leisurely or speedily for the subject remains the same, only the light changes. If the subject is set up close to a north window, even the change in light will be insignificant. The opportunity for lengthy study and painting without radical changes of light simplifies the painting problem.

Still life study should be started with only a few objects, simple planes and forms, each in a solid color without decoration of any kind. The following setup is easy and effective:

Cover a brown table with a piece of dark blue material. Push the material over to one

hang an ochre or mustard-colored piece of material. Further in, behind the middle part of the table, edging and slanting downwards against the mustard color, we hang a piece of paper painted unevenly with showcard color in a light bluish-lavender of the same value as the mustard-ochre color. At the extreme end of the other side, the rest of the background is filled out with a slanting piece of cardboard painted in a brownish-red, edging the blue-lavender. This way the whole background of the picture will be divided into three parts—each part in one distinctive color, starting with the largest section in ochre or mustard-yellow, the middle section in the light blue-lavender and ending with a triangular section of red-brown.

side, leaving half the table top free. Place a sheet of white typing paper diagonally across one corner of the table (see illustration).

On top of the white paper place a brick-colored flower pot holding a small plant consisting of three or four long, dark-green leaves.

So far we have only mild contrasts—the brick-red flower pot and the dark green; the dark blue against the brown table top. To strengthen the color scheme a trifle, we take a rectangular piece of yellow-orange paper, the size of a large, long envelope, and place one end of it over the dark blue and the other end over the brown. The blue will immediately look more intensely blue and the brown richer in tone, almost yellow-orange. We gradually intensify the color scheme by adding a few more contrasts.

Behind the uncovered end of the table, we

By the simple device of dividing the background into three different color sections, three more contrasts are gained that can be played against the colors already established in the color scheme. The mustard-yellow, which covers the largest part of the background behind the table, sets up a higher degree of intensity in the blue of the middle section and in the green leaves seen against the yellow.

A deep-red vase is placed on the dark-blue table cover. It should be tall enough to reach halfway up against the blue-lavender background. Put green leaves in the vase. Instead of a vase, a dark red candle can be set in a low candle holder; for a small active spot of color, make a funnel from bright yellow-green paper

Mustard

Dark Green

Brick Red

Purple Red
White
Brown

Red Brown
Blue
Lavender

Yellow Green

Yellow Green

Deep Red

Deep Red

Yellow
Orange
Dark Blue

and set it down on top of the candle.

Some small object, a toy or something similar in a deep purple-red, is placed beside the flower pot on the white paper to bridge the contrast between the white paper and the surrounding colors.

This completes the setup. It is now ready to be painted. Begin by painting the darkest colors first. The lightest colors are painted last. All colors are first painted lighter than the objects. They are then adjusted and made darker as the painting moves along.

Light colors are easily made darker without losing their brightness, but dark colors quickly become muddy in an attempt to lighten the color tone. White added to any color will almost immediately add a certain amount of gray. Before setting off colors on the canvas, try them out as color samples on painting paper. Then do a few quick preliminaries to make sure of a clean start. I cannot emphasize too often that when painting in oil colors it is important to begin with clear tones; distinctive tonality will surely follow.

The colors in the setup are not strong separate hues. Their individual strength is brought out fully in contrast with each other, as will be observed in the actual painting. The real aim in this exercise is to create a strongly drawn-together, warm tonal effect, in spite of the two cool colors. The dark blue, and the light, cold blue-lavender middle section of the background should, by simultaneous contrast, warm up sufficiently to give an over-all impression of warmth.

This suggested still life should be followed by others. The simplicity of the arrangement should be a challenge to the student. It demonstrates how commonplace objects of no special interest in themselves can be composed into a pleasing pictorial subject.

Here is an unusual still-life painting aid that is worth trying: a lump of white placed near objects in a composition. Sugar is one of the whitest substances commonly available and the contrast will give the painter the true value of the local color. This device was widely used by old-time painters in portrait painting and other similar close-up work as well as still life.

TULIPS IN BLUE VASE

A very simple flower arrangement in a vase, placed in flat light near a north window, is best for learning to paint the flower-piece. Choose a few flowers that have big clear forms and are closely related in color. Set the arrangement against as few accessories as possible.

The vase in this example was placed in front of a mirror, reflecting a wintry scene through a window. The ochre and rose mirror-frame and the wall were partly covered on each side by two white curtains, the two lines slanting downward. The effect of the square angle of the frame was thus softened and kept back.

The entire composition was first drawn in Rose Madder. Then the indigo-like, blue-black color of the vase, which accents the color scheme, was glazed in transparent Ultramarine Blue mixed with Cadmium Red.

The big red tulip, highlighted in Cadmium Yellow, deep, set the first color note in the bouquet. The three small, darker tulips in Crimson and Cadmium Red, painted in open brush strokes, had lighter shades set in with white-mixed local red. In order to emphasize painting in cold and warm, a larger tulip in brilliant Cadmium Yellow, deep, was added to bring out the cool shades in the reds.

Further outlining and broader shadows were drawn in rose color. This was allowed to dry completely before continuing the work.

Permanent Emerald Green is the basic green used in painting the leaves. Additional blue painted in the shadows and white-blue optic light on the top contrast with the Yellow Ochre of the reflected light underneath. These soft greens make the leaves a strong member of a color triad in green, yellow, and red.

Darker shades of the glazing color—the blue of the vase—were used to make stronger, darker shadows on the vase. To give it modeling and glass-transparency the green colors of the leaves and still darker accents in Crimson were painted alla prima into the wet glazing color-coat.

The cold gray reflections in the mirror were painted in Cobalt blue-white with Cadmium Red added in small portions. Against these light values of gray the vase and flowers stand out as a clear-cut design. The frosty color in the mirror had a darker shadow painted into it on the left side. This shadow, running over the frame, consists of the same general gray color, made deeper with more red added to the blue. Cadmium Yellow, deep, brushed into the corner of the frame and a bit at the top, is the only color contrast in the background variations of the cooler groups of white-grays.

The two curtain halves have blue, rose, and Ochre painted into the white in slanting brush strokes.

Between the two leaves sticking out to the left, an airy shade of a bluer value was slanted downward, and a warmer white over the edge of the curtain was repeated at the right side.

Warm shadows and cold lights over the white tablecloth finished the painting.

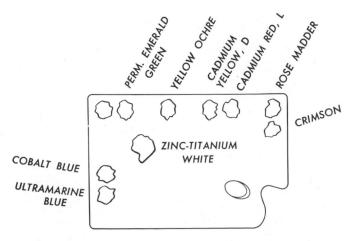

STILL LIFE AGAINST A RED BACKGROUND.

A linear arrangement of a few objects on a table can be easily composed and set up as an attractive still life, as in the painting shown here.

Ordinary utensils—bottles or boxes, cheap or expensive—are all equally effective. A simple arrangement of objects in good taste can be turned into a masterpiece.

This still life, set against red, is painted over a matchstick ink drawing, each part marked in lines drawn mostly as dots.

Over the ink drawing, red imprimatura is brushed out over the entire canvas in long strokes of streaky red.

Transparent damar varnish, diluted with

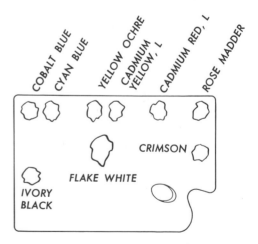

COBALT BLUE CYAN BLUE YELLOW OCHRE CADMIUM YELLOW, L CADMIUM RED, L ROSE MADDER

CRIMSON

FLAKE WHITE

IVORY BLACK

LANDSCAPE, STEP 4

LANDSCAPE, STEP 5

Two Farms

Mountain Village

NOVEMBER DAY

STILL LIFE AGAINST A RED BACKGROUND

SUNLIT FRONT YARD, STEP 4

SUNLIT FRONT YARD, STEP 5

PORTRAIT, LAST STEP

SUNSET

COOL WATER

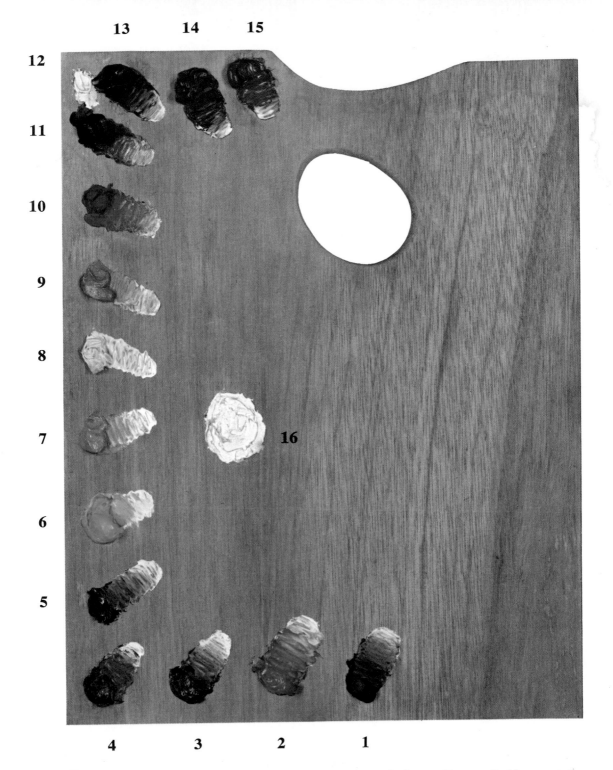

THE PALETTE SET UP WITH A FULL RANGE OF COLORS: 1. IVORY BLACK, 2. VIRIDIAN, 3. ULTRAMARINE BLUE, 4. COBALT BLUE, 5. CYAN BLUE, 6. PERMANENT EMERALD GREEN, 7. YELLOW OCHRE, 8. CADMIUM YELLOW, LIGHT, 9. CADMIUM YELLOW, DEEP, 10. CADMIUM RED, 11. ROSE MADDER, 12. FLAKE WHITE, 13. CRIMSON, 14. BURNT SIENNA, 15. VENETIAN RED, 16. ZINC WHITE.

SUMMER EVENING

STILL LIFE

medium #2, transforms the color into deep lustrous tonalities akin to the tones of some of the old masters.

Cadmium Red, light, darkened by Rose Madder, has a small quantity of Flake White mixed in to give body to the madder pigment and make it more stable in mixture. Reduced to flowing consistency, such a quickly drying color coat can be controlled with assurance. It is not possible to go back over the color before it has had time to dry completely. If you touch the undercoating with a wet brush while it is setting and in a half-dried state, the brush will lift the color right off. Should such a mishap occur, the only thing you can do is wait, and do the repair work on the dry imprimatura.

While the imprimatura is still freshly laid and wet, lighter areas in the drawing, such as the top of the box, the lamp, the edge of the plate, spots in the glasses, and so on, can be wiped lighter with a soft rag. Small spots can be rubbed with a small brush moistened in turpentine and lifted with tissue paper.

Areas in the red color can also be made lighter by brushing lightly over them.

Instead of repainting light areas in a lighter color, the same effect can be achieved by lightening them as described, in a free, bold manner. This is in keeping with the very free delineation of forms in the composition.

Stiff brushes that have worn short but still have a good edge are excellent tools for improvisation in laying imprimatura.

Take time to inspect the light and dark places before drawing the contours in black. While they are only slightly related to the ink drawing underneath, they are the clue to the most appropriate action to follow in contouring.

For free play in contouring, the lettering brush is held at arm's length at the end of the handle. A mixture of Ivory Black, Flake White and Cyan Blue produces a bluish black of considerable depth suitable for contour color. Like the undercoating, the black contour dries fast and is ready in a short time.

The separate objects are painted by a mere indication of their local color, the red playing through everywhere.

First, white is painted into the red around the edges of the objects. An extra stroke of heavier white is painted under the Chianti bottle. Moving up, the form of the bottle is modeled with Yellow Ochre and Cadmium Yellow, light. Background color, made darker with crimson, fills the bottle and the glasses with wine. The cork and the seal are marked in with a few deft brush strokes. The two lemons, in Cadmium Yellow and white, reflect the yellow into the two glasses. Behind, the blue-green handbag with a golden clasp is seen against the red. Thus, a so-called color triad of red, yellow and green creates a harmony against the total red tonality.

The old-fashioned coal oil lamp—in a neutral tone made of black and white—provides a restful interval in the color scheme. The ornamental base reflects the lemon yellow in the same way as the two glasses on the opposite side.

The bunch of grapes casts a cold purplish blue over its plate. A loose mixture of Cobalt Blue, white, and Rose Madder, with a touch of crimson added here and there, deepens the shadow thrown by the lamp.

The ochre rectangle on the box behind the grapes provides a light contrast which enlivens the blue in the grapes.

The key to this type of painting lies in the proper light touches of color over the red tonality, which comes through in light and dark in each object.

A full color reproduction of this painting will be found on the color spread.

If the basic painting rules and techniques discussed and demonstrated in this book have been well absorbed—not only read, but diligently practiced—then the student should be well on his way toward capable independent self-expression in painting. Book 3, the next book in the series, will introduce him to portrait painting and explore more advanced problems in landscape painting.

BOOK

3

Course

in Beginning

OIL PAINTING

Olle Nordmark

Introduction

The development of art is slow and painful. What was formerly thought to be the work of eccentrics or fanatics is recognized today as truth, expressed differently.

Truth is unchanging and timeless. Old truths in painting, learned by studying the old masters, are now acknowledged essentials in contemporary art.

In the past new forms of art often caused confusion among painters and misunderstanding, sometimes amounting to rage, among spectators and art critics. Upheavals and transitions often came about too abruptly, the artists saying too much too fast and explaining nothing. The bewildered public rejected new and unusual work that was later to be accepted and cherished. In France the works of such masters of color as Matisse, Roualt and Braque aroused storms of protest and indignation and the artists were labeled "Fauves," or wild beasts, by those who could not understand their drastic break with tradition.

Such is the development of art. At first a spurt, then it levels out until the new developments become an established, living part of everyday life; pictures that were formerly controversial become widely appreciated and no longer cause a hue and cry.

A deeply felt longing for the ability to create something in color on canvas is invariably the beginning of painting. Talent is indicated by the ability to discern light and dark (chiaroscuro), and cold and warm colors, in terms of setting them down with pigments.

Everything in painting is relative to the amount of training accumulated by study—with teachers, through books, or by self-training. Experience improves ability. To see and paint color-forms enclosed in the space of a composition is the object of study. Skill in handling painting materials is acquired through practice and intelligent understanding of the limitations as well as the possibilities of the materials. Progress in any painting method depends on the degree of the student's interest.

In this course, materials and methods are explained from a professional point of view in terms that can be understood by the beginner.

By following the instructions and doing the exercises the beginner can learn to paint which is more interesting and rewarding than just daubing.

Olle Nordmark

Chapter 1

Individuality

The problems of painting treated in this series are the essential ones of light and shadow, reflected light, and contrast, with specific reference to their behavior in Nature.

In Book 1 the problems treated are simple, with simple solutions and suitable examples. In Book 2 the problems taken up become more complicated. In this third book further complex aspects of painting are discussed.

The examples shown throughout this course are not meant to be slavishly copied. Not much would be gained from that except a familiarity with the feel of the materials. The examples are intended to point the way to a better understanding of the particular problems and principles of painting involved.

Although part of an example may be copied as a practical exercise in understanding the solution of the problem, the suggested procedure is to use each example and the accompanying text as a guide. To do this, select a subject with problems similar to those in the example and apply the principles you have learned to your own painting problems.

To lend variety to the painting exercises I have deliberately avoided using my own personal style of painting. It should not be your aim to paint like someone, but to learn from someone.

A good, free interpretation of a painting by Rembrandt which shows the student's own personal touch is far better than a painstaking imitative copy. Neither one is likely to approach the master's perfection, but the free interpretation would have individuality while the copy would be devoid of any life.

Every artist must find his own style of expressing himself in his painting and, having found it, must develop it to his ultimate ability. The student may be influenced by a variety of painting styles before he finds his own.

To gain a measure of freedom in style, some sculptors have tried modeling in total darkness. Painters trying this stunt usually end up with uncontrolled abstractions. However, such experimentation is valuable; even if it proves nothing more than that an idea is worthless, the painter has learned something.

There are many signs of an emerging personality, a growing individuality, in painting. An individual color scheme, a gracious or authoritative line, a tendency toward dark or light coloring, all these are signposts to be noted and analyzed.

It is difficult to tell at first what is genuinely your own, and what is borrowed. But the student who is honestly himself at all times will eventually succeed in putting the mark of his own personality on his work.

Knowing the history of art is a valuable aid to the student. The old painters whose works have delighted the eye for many generations teach us important lessons even though their subject matter and technique seem far removed from our own.

Museum reproductions and even inexpensive post card reproductions are fine for checking your work in progress against the works of the old masters. This is both exciting and revealing and has nothing to do with copying or imitating, but is rather a stimulus to creative impulse.

Helpful hints from a variety of sources, collected in keeping with the beginner's own tastes and interests, can lead him to a deeper understanding of his own work.

Before work on the canvas begins, a small loose drawing should be made of the subject to secure the original impression and to provide a means for checking the progress of the painting.

The names of the colors used in mixing the tones should be written down on the drawing,

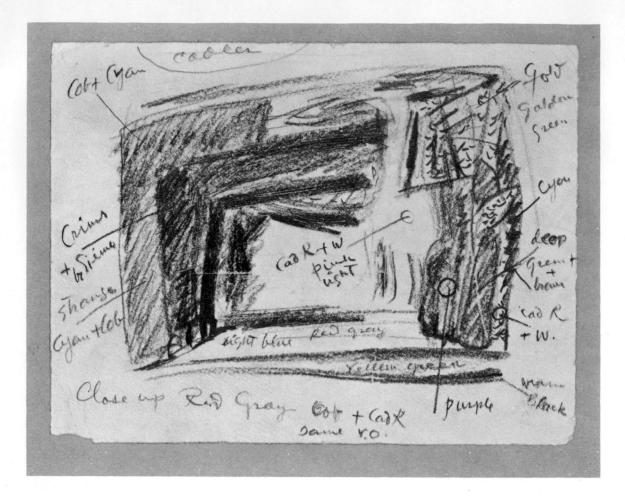

abbreviated and with pointers (*see illustration*). Recorded in this way the mixtures can be repeated at any time.

The old Spanish painter Zuloaga told a friend of mine that he rarely made a sketch of a scene. Instead of painting sketches, he carried a large notebook for making notes on the local colors, the light, and other details of a particular scene. He filled many notebooks with material for his paintings.

Chapter 2

Painting in Monochrome

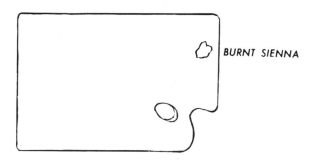

BURNT SIENNA

Painting a subject in one color is called painting in *monochrome*.

Painting in opaque or transparent monochrome has been practiced since the earliest periods of painting in oil colors.

Masterpieces in monochrome were often incorporated in architecture; they included murals, painted imitations of bas-reliefs, statuary, and architectural details designed to fool unwary eyes.

Grisaille is a kind of decorative painting in gray monochrome which was done by skilled craftsmen-decorators whose work found wide acclaim for its extreme realism. Anecdotes about these artists and their magic are still cherished tales.

Cool light and warm shadows, divided into highlight, glint, passage, general shadow, depth, and a still deeper accent, were skillfully handled by these wizards of the paint pots. Theirs were mechanically divided shadings, but gave the illusion of reality. In the allegorical grisaille panel they often added, as a gesture, a painted shadow thrown by the painted object itself. These paintings were so realistic that the saying was "you could hang your hat on the unicorn's horn."

Many of the finest painters of various per-

iods tried their hand at monochromatic painting, and many fine examples of the gray tonality have come from their workshops, sometimes only in the two abstracts, black and white. This abstract pair of colors has come back in contemporary painting with a bang. However, present-day monochromatic painting is usually done in a warm transparent brown, a brown with a red or orange cast. On a pure white canvas ground this warm-colored painting stands out in a surprisingly varied richness of nuances.

Pure black, primarily a cool color, does not register in such a variety of nuances on white. The white, cool in itself, does not provide the necessary contrast.

Opaque black, on the other hand, contrasts strongly when painted straight against pure white, as in modern abstract painting. Here it functions with an entirely different meaning in its extreme exaggeration of power.

Monochrome is an easy approach to portrait painting. Every beginner would like to be able to do a portrait; the first requirement is, of course, the ability to draw a likeness.

The monochrome study of a head, reproduced on the following page, is at the beginner's level.

THE OLD PAINTER

This portrait study is executed in monochrome Burnt Sienna and only turpentine thinner is used to give the Sienna transparency.

To duplicate the exercise, first draw the head with a few light charcoal lines and follow with light drawing in Sienna. Keep to a free, light-handed style in all the drawing. Do not use pencil as this would bleed into the canvas ground and could not be removed. After the color outlining is dry, slap off surplus charcoal with a rag or rub it lightly with a kneaded eraser.

Use sable hair brights and ox hair brushes for painting. Lay the color smooth and flowing without brush marks or rubbing off of partly dried areas.

The Sienna and turpentine color is quick-setting and each application must be allowed to dry thoroughly before the next coat is laid over it; if wet brush strokes touch partly dried under-layers they will lift out the coat underneath.

All dark parts in each area must be painted twice to get darkness without opaque heaviness, otherwise they will lose luster and turn hard-looking, with sharp edges.

Light spots are left unpainted, then covered thinly at the end of the work. Small spots that look too dark or heavy can be fixed with a small brush moistened in turpentine and rubbed over the spot; then the loosened color can be lifted out with blotting paper.

The painting should look clear and lustrous.

Chapter 3

The Approach to Painting

Beginners are inclined to think that experienced painters get their effects easily, without travail. This is not so. Great masters are great because they are willing to take infinite pains and do the work over again an indefinite number of times at any stage of the painting. Willingness to erase, or to start all over again on a clean painting surface is essential to good painting, whether you are a beginner or an artist of established reputation.

Karl Isakson, an outstanding Swedish colorist known for his exact precision of tone, often discarded as many as 30 paintings of one subject before he was willing to show anyone his canvas. The Danish painter, Edward Weil, who also delved deeply into the problems of color, destroyed painting after painting that did not come up to his high personal standards. Although the color harmonies in his later paintings are superb, very few satisfied his own critical eye.

No effort should be considered "too much trouble" when you are trying to solve a painting problem. There is no sleight-of-hand magic in painting. Satisfaction in painting depends on how much work you are willing to do. You can get much pleasure and the excitement of self-expression long before you are an accomplished artist if you do not try to over-reach yourself by attempting ambitious projects before you are ready for them.

Confronted with the formidable problem of color—and painting begins and ends with color—the beginner needs guidance all the way. I have planned exercises, given suggestions for procedures, and discussed a variety of techniques in order to clarify as many areas as possible in a course of this kind.

Certain aspects of nature can only be represented by color, and this must be made clear to the beginner before he can paint effectively.

He must also learn the technical procedures and color mixtures that will help him paint the picture he has in mind.

Texture, which is the physical imprint left on the painting surface by the brush or painting knife, is the strictly personal marking of the painter. As his skill improves he can add effects by the judicious use of texture, but too much emphasis on this can interfere with the free flow of the picture idea.

Lack of discipline in painting, as in anything else, leads to chaos. Only technical knowledge will give you true freedom. If you master the techniques presented in this course, you will understand the basic natural laws of light and color and will be able to apply them freely in your own way.

Before you get ready to paint you should do a few rapid idea sketches in pencil or charcoal, or a small rough in oils, no more than a color notation.

Some people have so many ideas for paintings that they hardly know which one to choose. Others must search for ideas.

One of the best ways to stir the creative forces is to take a walk, in the countryside or along the city streets, sketching casually as something appeals to your imagination.

Do not try too hard when casting about for a painting idea. Do not force the creative mechanism. If the artist's mind is clear and unhurried, it will usually generate ideas inspired by something that catches his fancy.

The door to the mind opens inward; the beginner in his eagerness may shut it tight.

One artist may perceive an idea first as color; another may be interested primarily in form. Some will have a definite picture of the whole painting in mind when they wake up ir the morning.

An idea that has become elusive and diffused should be forgotten entirely for a while. Sleep on it. It may come back the next day, fresh and clear.

The artist's hand holds and moves the brush, but his mind paints the picture.

I know an artist, a soldier with both arms amputated, who paints by holding a brush between his teeth. The excitement of seeing the painting in his mind emerge in colors on a canvas is certainly greater for this man than it could possibly be for most of us. He paints for fun.

Painting is fun, and the more you know, the more fun it will be.

Of course it takes patience and application to make progress, but if you use these books properly for self-training you can have a lot of fun as you learn. I have tried to make the in-structions clear and keep the exercises simple and interesting so that at every stage of learning you will be doing something that is a satisfying accomplishment.

Substituting other colors for the colors set out on the palette will defeat the purpose of my systematic teaching. Exploring the chromatic possibilities of the palette according to the instructions is the best possible way to use this course for self-education. Remember that many of the world's most renowned painters were self-taught.

Each step in painting a picture must look complete in itself. If each stage is carried out with this in mind there will be no falling apart of the tonality at a latter stage, and the progress of the work will be easier to keep under control.

Chapter 4

About Drawing

Painting is drawing with a brush. This profound truth has been handed down from Michelangelo himself and the sooner the beginner realizes its basic importance the sooner he will understand the whole subject of painting. Its essential quality cannot be stressed too much. Drawing not only forms the bones of the painting—its underlying structure—but drawing continues until the last brush stroke is on the canvas. When the beginner acquires drawing facility with the brushes, he is on his way to becoming a painter.

Drawing is felt everywhere in a picture; it disappears into the color only to reappear. A single line may sharpen a value or give more depth to a shadow. Pictures can be painted entirely in line drawing, and there are seemingly endless uses for drawing in color or in monochrome. Drawing helps to unify the painting into a free-flowing composition. It must be used as the chief support of the painting throughout.

The beginner should practice drawing constantly. He should do innumerable drawings with pencil, charcoal, or brush, to loosen up and get the "feel."

Every kind of drawing is valuable practice whether you draw in a sketchbook, notebook, on a pad, or render a fine finished drawing on high quality paper; whether you use pencil, charcoal, silverpoint, pen and ink, or brushes. Paint brushes and charcoal are mentioned throughout the course. Here is a brief descriptive listing of a few other drawing mediums:

Pencils can be black, sepia, or sanguine. The French Conté sticks and crayon pencils are well known and widely used.

Silverpoints, old-time drawing instruments much used in Leonardo da Vinci's period, are still available. This instrument consists of a silver rod or a piece of silver wire held by a pencil lead holder such as is carried by most art stores. This is an interesting method of drawing and not too expensive to try. Silverpoints leave lines of soft beauty on special white coated paper. After the silver begins to tarnish the tone becomes deeper. Formerly, silverpoint drawings were made on paper covered with a white paste made by mixing a white powder with Gum Arabic; now a special coated paper bound into sketchbooks of English manufacture is available in some art stores.

Drawing pens are available in a large assortment of shapes designed for making every kind of line from the finest hairline to broad ribbon lines. Special artists' fountain pens that hold a large amount of ink are good. These have a number of different points to choose from. There may be some ball-points with which you can draw an uninterrupted line—I haven't found one.

The *reed pen,* another time-honored drawing instrument, is still available. Leonardo da Vinci and Rembrandt used the reed pen for rapid sketches with astounding results. Many of Rembrandt's most highly prized drawings were made with the scantiest strokes of the reed. Vincent van Gogh did his magnificent ink drawings of the Saintes-Maries with a reed pen—they are brilliant examples of what a simple, modest drawing implement in the hand of a great artist can accomplish.

My own personal ink drawing tool is the lowly kitchen match stick. Used as it comes from the box, it produces a thick, bold line; or it can be whittled down to a point to produce a fine line. The wood, being soft, is slightly absorbent and holds the ink well. The lines have slightly ragged edges which give a distinctive quality quite different from lines produced by pens and brushes.

Try some drawings with a match stick. Wind sticky tape around the match stick to keep it from wobbling. Then get a good firm grip on it with your thumb and index finger and start your sketch. It's fun, and it will increase your drawing flexibility.

There are many other drawing mediums—crayons, pastels, fountain brushes, Chinese and Japanese writing brushes, and so on. You will discover them for yourself as time goes by.

Experimenting with a variety of mediums is a good idea. You will eventually find the ones that are just right for you.

I can highly recommend Ernest W. Watson's "Course in Pencil Sketching," (Reinhold), for factual information about implements and techniques.

A bench near a playground is a wonderful spot for action sketching. Children at play make invaluable models, but don't attempt anything more than an indication of the movement—simply draw a series of lines to show the changing positions of the fast-moving little arms and legs. Catching the momentary pose, the shifting action, is the object of this kind of drawing. The idea is to train the eye and make the hand follow. If you look directly at the model your eyes only need to shift from model to paper and you can follow every move.

Collect sketches of all kinds in handy pocket-size books for later use. Unlined school composition books are very good for sketching,

provided the paper is of reasonably good quality. You will need only the simplest tools: a sharp pocket knife; erasers; soft, medium, and hard pencils; and a small box of children's colored crayons including bright yellow, bright and rose red, dark vivid green, a clear blue, and black.

As a companion piece to your pocket-size sketchbook, provide yourself with a good ruled notebook of about the same size, for written notes.

And what will be revealed when you have filled the two books in your pocket? The work

you have done will disclose the character of your personal creative impulses; you will know the joy of seeing what you have found out for yourself, uninfluenced by anything but your own response to the world around you. All this will help you understand the trend of your own talents. Hold on to what seems to be right and true for you and develop your talents in that direction. Too many beginners become confused by the many possibilities in the field of art, and scatter their efforts without a clear-cut aim.

Whatever the extent of your talent, it must be nurtured and exercised regularly, otherwise it will shrink and grow stale. An artistic temperament does not mean sitting down and waiting for inspiration to flash a message on the mental screen. This is a very uncertain occupation indeed. You will make far more progress by painting or drawing for a short time every day than by working furiously for long periods only now and then.

Chapter 5

Drawing the face

The easiest way to draw a full face looking straight ahead is to first draw three pencil guide lines to be erased later. The lines are as follows:

One, a vertical line the length of the face, drawn to divide the face in half. Two, a horizontal line the width of the face, drawn across the vertical at a point representing the center of the eyes. Three, a horizontal line the width of the mouth, drawn across the vertical at the proper point.

With the help of these three guide lines, proportions and the placement of the features within the face oval are easy to control. (On a face turned sideways, the guiding lines for eyes and mouth must be drawn in perspective.)

Eyes in the drawing are placed at the same level as the artist's own eyes during work on the painting. The width of one eye from corner to corner is equal to the distance between the eyes.

Do the actual drawing with a pointed charcoal stick. Check it in a mirror from time to time. The reverse image will reveal such mistakes

as wrong proportions or any differences in the two halves of the face.

When you are satisfied with the drawing, slap the surplus charcoal off with a rag, being careful to keep the drawing itself intact. Outline it with Rose Madder mixed with a minute part of Flake White. Thin the color with plain turpentine and use a lettering brush as the drawing tool.

The drawing in color also needs to be checked with the mirror from time to time to

detect errors. It is important that eyes, nostrils, ears, and mouth are in correct relation to each other; and that their true position is kept intact on the guide lines.

Let the finished outlining dry hard enough to permit erasure of the pencil guide lines and excess charcoal without smearing the color. Do the erasing with a kneaded eraser.

Willingness to do all the seemingly unimportant small chores will produce a drawing that will be a helpful guide from the beginning to the end of a painting.

Chapter 6

A Portrait Step-by-Step

The "shadowless" face is a contemporary style in both portraiture and fashion art. This painting of a girl is an example of such a face devoid of dark shadows and hard side light.

The sculptural style, with sharp contrasts of light and shadows, will be taken up later on. After the student has gained experience and insight by doing less involved problems, he can tackle the complexities of bright light, deep shadow, and reflected light—light from both sides and shadow running down the middle.

In portraiture, heavy demands are made on the ability to draw a likeness. The painter must continue to draw with the brushes until the picture is finished. In addition, the elusive skin tones must be reproduced on canvas.

I have chosen this simple shadowless face as a beginning exercise because it is both the easiest and the soundest method of learning the fundamentals of portrait painting. The painting procedure will be explained in five illustrated steps after some general instructions.

Some of the mysteries of light and color over the skin can be solved by learning how to paint cool color over warm color, and cool light over warm shadow. Painting in successive coats of cold and warm is the fastest way to build form. The generally accepted use of transparent shadow, semi-covering middle tone, and fairly opaque highlight is probably the best way to get good results in painting flesh tints, and in depicting the human face and figure.

Successive coats of color in cold and warm create the transparent depth of the human skin and usually make repainting of middle tones or passages unnecessary. The passage tones, especially, seem to create themselves effortlessly over the margin between light and shadow, as will be fully explained in the fifth step.

Holding freshness of color from the beginning to the end is probably the hardest part of painting the human features. However, by avoiding the use of black entirely, the pitfalls of heavy, drab shadows can be fairly well eliminated.

The palette is set up with seven colors and the two whites—Flake White for the underpainting, and Zinc White for the finishing or top layers. The range of this palette is sufficient for any type of realistic portrait painting.

Set out from left to right are: Ultramarine Blue; Yellow Ochre, light; Cadmium Yellow, light; Cadmium Yellow, deep; Rose Madder; Crimson; and Burnt Sienna. The two whites are in the center. Always repeat the same order in setting up the palette so you will be able to find the color you want automatically.

Only gum turpentine combined sparingly with Flake White is used to make the underpainting lean. In the finishing surface coat a combination of Zinc White and the #1 painting medium (1 part raw linseed oil to 2½ parts of gum turpentine) is used.

A detailed pencil drawing of the subject is necessary as preliminary work for the sake of simplifying the actual work with brushes and colors.

For early attempts at portrait painting it is advisable to avoid a full-scale portrait, although a fairly large head should be tried. If the size is too small the usual brushes will be too large and the result will be a cramped style and a messy daub. As a practical beginning, I advise you to make the head in this exercise at least 6 inches high, from chin to top of head.

The brushes necessary to duplicate the exercise are: four *brights,* #4, #5, #6, and #7; two *flats*, #1 and #2; two small *rounds*, #0 and #1; one flat and one round sable hair brush, #1. Backgrounds are laid in with ¾ inch brights of the inexpensive "student" grade.

For portrait painting, flat brushes that have worn round, or flats specially made with round corners, instead of the usual square-cornered bristle, are well adapted for drawing in color. Used either broadside or edgewise, they work easily as drawing tools.

Professional portrait painters work with slow-drying mediums or color mixtures which facilitate painting wet in wet, alla prima, as much as possible. I would not advise the student to tackle such a method at first for only expert handling of the materials can produce good results. The inexperienced will paint himself a headache.

Much better results and wider experience can be obtained by working with the faster-drying raw linseed oil and gum turpentine medium. Sureness of approach should be mastered before reaching out for techniques calling for professional dexterity. Spontaneity of performance comes with acquired skill, not from some particular method regardless of how tempting it may look at first glance. It is better to improve upon what one has learned and to improvise from time to time.

Set up the canvas on the easel at eye level to keep the features under constant control. Step back after every other brush stroke and look at your work. Hold the brush at the end of the handle and paint at arm's length to overcome rigidity and that insecure feeling.

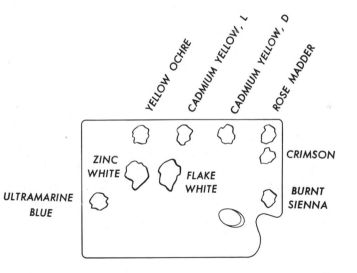

Step one. Transfer your detailed full-scale pencil drawing to the canvas either by direct outlining in charcoal or by printing off the drawing from a tracing, as explained in detail in Book 1. Surplus charcoal is dusted off, or lightened with a kneaded eraser.

Outline the drawing in Rose Madder mixed with a little Flake White and thinned with turpentine. Use the round sable brush and a broader bristle brush. The color should be of water-color consistency. Mistakes can be erased with a soft rag moistened in turpentine. This outlining will generally dry within a half hour. The small addition of Flake White sets the color quickly and hardens it so that it is pleasant to paint over.

All types of underpainting must have a lean, meager quality in order to dry out fast and stay hard after drying; only Flake White ground in raw linseed oil should be used as an additive. Slow-drying whites may take several weeks to dry; they do not have hardening characteristics. Painting over color surfaces of this type could result in loosening and softening of the underlayer, and eventual cracking. White lead, Flake White, and Cremnitz White if ground in slow drying oils also behave in this way.

After the outlining is dry, the hair, eyes, and lips are painted in flat forms, using the same Rose Madder, Flake White color mixture.

The warm shadow on the face and breast,

moving down to the neck opening of the blouse, is painted next. This shadow continues in drawing in the last step. The shadow is rendered warm by mixing Burnt Sienna with Yellow Ochre and a touch of Flake White. The ever-present danger of over-modeling and rounding of shadow forms must be watched particularly in the first three steps.

Turpentine thinner is the only medium used until the last step.

Step two. Rose Madder and Cadmium Yellow, deep, are painted out over the hair in a thin transparent coat, producing a rich reddish tone. Ultramarine Blue and Flake White, lightly mixed directly on the canvas with the broad brush, are painted loosely over the background.

Such half-covering color-coats will retain their airy transparency in the overpainting to follow, and will not burden the painting with the deadening effect of a heavy, numb surface.

Step three. Here attention is again given to the coiffure. More depth is set into the shadows; avoid deliberate modeling at this point by painting in broad strokes of Burnt Sienna, leaving the highlights of the hair untouched.

The forms of the face and neck, inside the flat shadow, are also painted in flat areas up to and alongside the shadow. The hue of the skin—Rose Madder and Cadmium Yellow, light, warmed up a little with Yellow Ochre and con-trolled with Flake White—becomes part of the lean undertone that is important in the finishing step.

Painting the flat forms only up to a certain point will leave the painter ample freedom and ease for further development of the form later. Handling the problem of modeling in this manner eliminates endless and fruitless overpainting which usually ends up in a murky, undecided tonality.

Step four. Deeper shadows and some modeling of the waves and curls in the coiffure can begin at this stage, but care must still be taken not to overdo the modeling and throw away valuable possibilities for light and shadow in the final stage. Depth in the shadow of the hair is easily put in with Ultramarine Blue, some white, and Burnt Sienna; again, the highlight area should be kept as free from heavy paint as possible. The red Sienna underneath should be allowed to show through the shadow tone as a contrasting hue. Alternating strokes of Rose Madder and Sienna set into the blueish-Sienna depth will further enrich this deep shadow tone.

Red-orange made of Rose Madder and Cadmium Yellow, deep, is painted in a light value over the iris of the eyes, and over the lips.

The lobes of the ears and the pearls should not be overlooked. Add a shade of rose over the ear lobes and white over the pearls.

It must be kept in mind that undertoning is not intended to play an over-all role. The next stage—the so-called passages in a cool gray tone over the underlying warmth—will probably need some pondering upon to be understood correctly. A light gray mixture of Ultramarine Blue and Yellow Ochre, subdued with Rose and Flake White, is painted in vertical brush strokes, thinly, over the flesh that is in the light. Darker gray passage tones are automatically produced as the forms are rounded off into the warmer shadows by continuing the light gray in a half-covering fashion into parts of the shadow. During this blending procedure, places here and there should be left entirely free of the light gray, to give plasticity.

Using vertical strokes over the flesh and the passages avoids overdone rounding of the form. The treatment with gray over the flesh is the same for every part of the body in all figure painting. The result should be the transparent, half-covering pearly gray seen in shimmering half-lights over the human body. It all hinges on the mechanical color treatment—once this has been mastered, it has endless possibilities of form-building in the overpainting to follow.

The background-blue lightened with white makes a suitable undertone for the blouse.

In controlling the underpainting with Flake White, you will find that stubby brushes will spread the color with a minimum use of thinner. Slippery, glossy colors are next to impossible to work over. Lean undercoating in meager color has all the possibilities needed for successful work and safe technical procedure.

The old-timers axiom "fat over lean," as well as alternating cool color over warm and warm color over cool, still holds true in painting in every technique from fresco to oil colors.

Step five. (See the color insert on page 25 for the finished painting.) If the beginner has followed the first four steps, he will have gained a broad basic knowledge of portrait painting. He should by now have some understanding of the complexity of light, shadow, and passages over the face, the use of cold and warm color, transparent shadow and opaque light, and semi-transparent passage tones—all elements important to the modeling of features.

There are no set rules for producing a fine painting; there are only natural laws and fundamental principles. After that it is up to the painter. Knowing the simplest basic techniques of handling the building materials of painting is generally enough for a good start.

In the finishing stage, the slower drying Zinc White is employed instead of the fast-drying Flake White. Flake White is used only in minute additions to Rose Madder and Crimson as a stabilizing element. Both the Zinc and Flake White must be the kind that is ground in raw linseed oil.

The background blue (Ultramarine Blue, with Zinc White instead of Flake White) is

broken to a faint shade of violet by adding Crimson. This shade is used to tone the background around the head, following the form of the head.

The white blouse and the face against the toned background are painted next, with a minimum of sculptural modeling. Soft shadows and softly blended light bring out the head in silhouette against the blue. Light gray is laid over the blouse and pure white highlights are painted in. The gray is made from complementary blue-red controlled with white. Such grays will stand in accurate relationship to the blue and the warm colors of the face.

The flesh tint is painted at this point. Final finishing of the face is left until the very end. The local color of the skin should have youthful freshness.

A small heap of the general skin color is made up using white, Rose Madder and Cadmium Yellow, light. The pinkish flesh on the forehead is approximately the general tone of the whole face, made a bit browner by adding a little Yellow Ochre.

The flesh tint is put on to only half cover the gray underneath—which should be as dry and hard as possible—and only partly covers the shadow.

The darkest value, the hair, which is important to the whole of the face, is painted next.

Shining reflections of light over the waves that were spaced out in the underpainting are now brought into balance by carefully modeling the roundness of the waves, using Sienna in thin transparency. Half tones are set directly into the wet Sienna, using Ochre and blue. Individual locks of hair and highlights are lightened with white, and are drawn with as much precision and accuracy as possible. If corrections are needed, scraping with the palette knife and painting over again is the only remedy.

Modeling of the waves is completed with blue-black, Sienna, white, and Ultramarine Blue, laid close to the shiny highlights and into the deepest shadows. Even deeper depths are created in this dark color by setting in stronger accents in Rose Madder, Sienna, and blue. Cooler shades of the same color, made by adding small portions of white, are necessary where contrasts in cold and warm are needed.

After the hair is finished the earlobes are painted in a rose-pink shade of the flesh tint.

The two pearls are done in transparent shades of yellow, rose, and blue. These three colors create the so-called pearl-gray. In lighter values, with white, they give the tone for the reflection of light over the surface. Each pearl, painted in pink-yellow and rose-gray, hangs from a narrow golden chain with gold fasteners attached to the ears. Yellow Ochre, Cadmium Yellow, deep, and Sienna will produce the golden metal tones.

Now it is time to complete the face; it still has a minimum of sculptural modeling throughout. Work starts with the eyes. The eyes should always be painted in as soon as possible to impart life to the features. They establish vital expression in the face, which makes a great deal of difference in painting a likeness.

Painting of the eyes should be alla prima, that is, wet in wet, as much as possible to preserve luster and freshness. A golden Sienna tone is used for the iris, darkened around the rim with Ultramarine Blue. Reflections of warm light, deep inside the iris, are painted around the black pupil. This black is made by mixing blue-rose and enough Sienna to render the black neutral. The whites of the eyes are shaded in blue. Form is painted into the blue with pure white, wet in wet, so that the white pigment literally seems to float.

The pinpoint reflections on the pupils are two small blobs of thick white lifted up on the tip of a #4 round sable hair brush and set off in the exact place on each pupil.

The lips may need close study before they are attempted. The upper lip is shaded with rose-white over orange-red; the lower lip is shaded in cooler Crimson. Between the lips, a narrow line shapes the parting and there is a faint outlining of the Cupid's bow. Highlights in the shiny moisture on the lower lip are set into the finishing tone, wet in wet.

Eyebrows take careful consideration before being drawn in color. If they are not handled carefully they are apt to cause changes in the face, upsetting the likeness and the form of the forehead in a most disturbing manner. Should the likeness be lost, adjustments can be made with the flesh tint. The direction of the hairs in the eyebrows is interesting and a close study is recommended.

The upper eyelids are tinted dark blue and the shadows in the folds are sharpened. The shaping of the eyes, as well as the eyelashes, is done in blue-black mascara tone. These are all elements of the likeness.

Warmer shadows over the lower lid and brown on the eyelashes produce contrasts bridging over to the warmer color tones below.

Final modeling of the face is begun by reddening the cheeks with Rose Madder and white in half-covering shades. The nose, the connecting feature between the eyes and the mouth, is shaped in thin painting with the flesh tint over the shadow. Nostrils are drawn in Sienna and blue, the openings in darker markings. Here again one must be careful not to spoil the hard-earned likeness.

Strengthening of the warm shadow is completed in Sienna and Ochre. Warmer reflections under the chin are achieved by strokes of reflected color in Cadmium Yellow, deep. With variations, the shadow is deepened in the same manner over the neck and the breast.

After the shadows are properly balanced, cool optic light is painted out over the higher areas—the forehead, the chin, and the nose.

Warm highlights are added over the tip of the nose, around the nostrils and edging the mouth. For this, mixtures of white, Cadmium Yellow, light, and a barely discernible part of Rose Madder are used.

Finally, soft shades, light and cool, in tones made from the cold Crimson, are very effective in the highlighted moisture of the skin. Since areas like these are broader than the high points of the bone structure, broad brushes are best.

This finishes the portrait of a girl. A full color reproduction of the finished portrait is shown on the color spread.

Chapter 7

Portrait Exercises

STUDY OF A SMILING FACE

After the experience gained by doing the preceding exercise, this animated face should not be difficult. The artist must keep alert to the importance of maintaining a likeness from the first brush stroke right through until the final highlight is placed.

Painting the human face by using some simplified system like undertoning over a color-outlined drawing is of real help in beginning portraiture. Here a light undertoning is used, made of Rose Madder and Yellow Ochre with the usual small part of Flake White added to the Madder. Zinc White, carefully pressed in with the palate knife, little by little, adds body. Medium #1 is the diluent. Both the Zinc White and Medium #1 are used with restraint. The undertoning is done with ¾ inch brights.

Brush marks are left in to give a feeling of looseness to the surface, but open streaks showing the priming should not be allowed. This is in direct opposition to imprimatura laid in streaky brush strokes.

Before applying the undertoning, a final check is made to be sure that no pencil lines are present. Some pencil blacks, if painted over with thin oil color, bleed out, increase in depth, or otherwise prove to be a real nuisance. Indelible pencils are disastrous.

Begin the painting by modeling the waves in the hair. Use a wide brush and loose strokes. Shadows in Burnt Sienna are followed by Cadmium Red, light, and Cadmium Yellow, deep. Thin these out to the same consistency as the undertoning in order to get natural lightness in the hair.

Finish the waves in darker and lighter red-orange with deeper Sienna shadows put in with the flexible sable brushes and the lettering brush.

The eyebrows are finished in color drawing in the same tones as the hair.

The red-orange of the hair and the brows is the main constant in the color scheme. Therefore the two cooler contrasts—the greenish-gray eyes and the cool rose lips—are painted next.

The eyes should be painted wet in wet. White-mixed Permanent Emerald Green is laid in transparency over the iris. Gray is used to shade and model, painting directly into the wet green color, more or less as a contour floating out over the green. Viridian-Crimson black pupils are centered in the gray-green iris and finished with a small reflected glint. Use the gray of the iris thinly to cover the whites of the eyes, rounding them off and outlining the upper eyelid.

The folds of the upper lid and the eyelashes are drawn in Ochre Sienna. Deepen the shadows in the corners of the eyes.

The nostrils are drawn in the same soft, warm shadows used around the eyes.

To maintain the moist freshness of color over the mouth, painting wet in wet is a must. Rose Madder and Cadmium Red, light, is laid over the upper lip. The lower lip is modeled in Crimson and white, thinly, in soft painting. The dark shadows in the corners of the mouth are drawn in with Crimson and Sienna.

Pure white is used for the gleaming white of the teeth. Drawing is done with Sienna, and at the same time the upper lip is outlined in a Sienna shadow.

A sharp glint of white set into the right places on the lips creates the illusion of moisture.

A light shadow-color made of Sienna and Cadmium Red, light, is employed wherever shadows are present. Make up enough of this to last throughout the painting. The uniformity of the shadow color brings order and balance to the

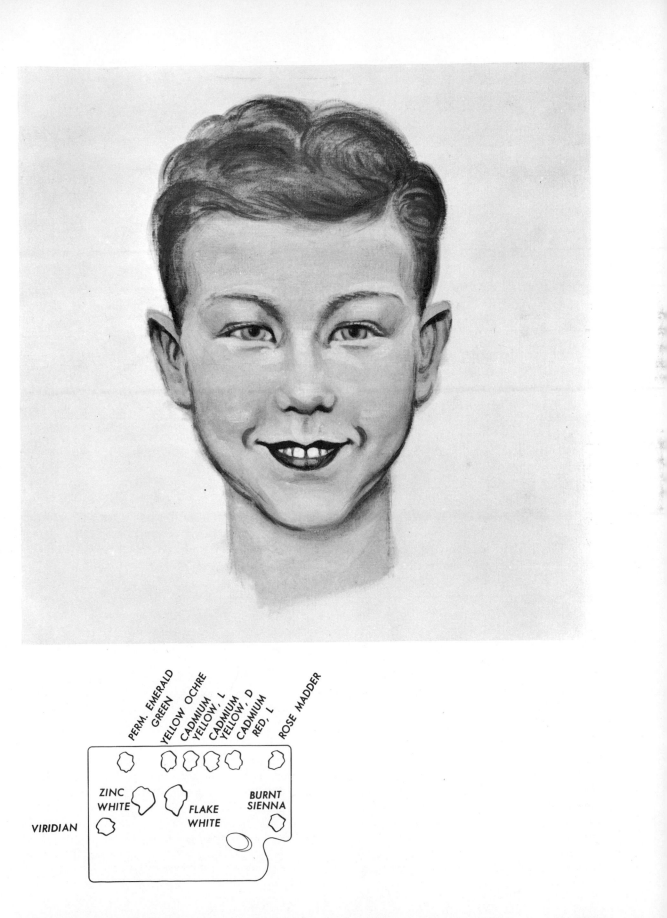

PERM. EMERALD
GREEN

YELLOW OCHRE

CADMIUM
YELLOW, L

CADMIUM
YELLOW, D

CADMIUM
RED, L

ROSE MADDER

ZINC
WHITE

FLAKE
WHITE

BURNT
SIENNA

VIRIDIAN

139

face with a minimum of work.

Translucent rosiness tinged with red is applied to the cheeks and ears in light, broad strokes and flat modeling. Ochre is set in where the color takes on a warmer value. A very small amount of white makes the color semi-transparent.

Rounding and strengthening of form is done as one moves along with the work.

At this stage the likeness should be checked in the mirror. Mistakes are corrected by drawing, in the shadow tone.

For the light over the features use Rose Madder mixed with white and a barely noticeable amount of Cadmium Yellow, light. This important color is also made up in sufficient quantity to last through the entire painting. The shade can be made darker or lighter at will, without disturbing the original color, by moving a small part aside with the palette knife. Nothing can be more exasperating than running out of a certain color tone at a critical moment, and endless re-mixings of the large tones will soon throw the whole painting out of kilter; it is always difficult to find the original color tone again.

The light must not show a sharp, abrupt difference in value against the general tone of the face; it should be only mildly lighter and cooler in tone.

The lightest highlights are put in last. For these use the light tone with a little more of the Cadmium Yellow, light.

I have purposely excluded deeper shadows and the very highest light, which is the glint. The beginner should find these for himself by looking at a live face. He will find the glint as small shining lights on the moisture of the highest parts of the features.

Throughout the painting the general color is kept light and bland, in keeping with the translucent lines of a young face.

After the painting is dry, the healthy outdoor color of the skin is added by glazing—but first a thin coat of retouching varnish (*see Book 4*) must be applied over the dry painting. The retouching varnish evens out the absorbent mat colors and the shining non-absorbent ones, thus eliminating ruinous spottiness. After the varnish is dry, the surface is ready for color glazing.

For this, use a straight coat of Rose Mad-

der and Yellow Ochre, with perhaps a touch of Cadmium Yellow, deep. An exceedingly thin glaze should give the effect of the sun without a dark sunburned look. Do not touch the eyes or the mouth. The hair is adjusted in the same way as the face.

Puddles and runs in the glazing color can be avoided by doing the glazing while the painting lies flat on a table. Steady strokes from a wide, soft brush should paint out the glaze without backing-in on color that is starting to set up.

STUDY OF A HEAD

By far the fastest route to satisfying results in oil painting is to work methodically for the sole purpose of gaining technical knowledge and painting experience. The beginner must use every opportunity to observe, draw and practice exercises in color harmony. He will do more for himself this way than by listening half-heartedly to lectures and then trying to apply what he has heard.

I do not mean that teachers are not necessary or important. They are. But study, without the hard "homework" to go with it, is not enough.

I cannot emphasize too often that all painting starts with drawing, and continues by drawing with brushes in colors. The ability to draw well is all-important. To draw what one actually sees when looking at a model is particularly important in face and figure work. For instance, observe a head. Notice that one side is usually quite different from the other. An old teacher of mine used to say that it is just as hard to find a head with two halves alike as it is to find two heads alike!

Spontaneity in grasping what is seen, and the technical "know-how" to transfer the impression to the canvas are the very essence of face and figure painting.

In this exercise we take up the study of a head that has more modeling and shading than the simple front faces in the two preceding exercises. The description follows the painting sequence from the beginning to the point where the finishing would start. The finishing stage is left out to emphasize the earlier methods of procedure. The next exercise will present a completely finished head in strong light and shadow.

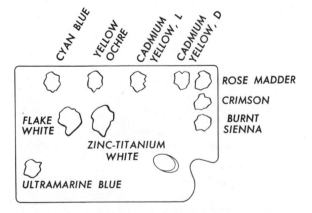

Eyebrows and eyes in their correct relation to the nose, and the nose in its relation to the mouth are drawn with as few lines as possible, but the ear, ornamental and complicated, demands a close check in drawing. Hairline, neck, and the folds in the jacket are drawn in a more general way.

Before beginning brush drawing, check the charcoal drawing in the mirror for mistakes in proportion.

Generally the first brush drawing of form is done with a turpentine-thinned color tone—a neutral warm black, brown, or greenish color depending on whether a cold or warm color scheme is planned. For the paintings reproduced here I mixed Yellow Ochre and Cyan Blue and neutralized the resulting green shade with Rose Madder; to set the color quickly, I added a small part of Flake White.

The first steps are covered in the first illustration. The head is drawn in its position on the canvas with only a few light lines in charcoal. Mistakes are either slapped off with a soft rag, or picked off with a kneaded eraser.

On the average canvas priming, this type of drawing color will dry quickly, and work can proceed almost immediately.

When the brush drawing in color-tone is completed, it is checked again with the mirror.

The second illustration shows the half-finished painting.

For the actual painting in color, Medium #2 is used. This medium is best for the beginner as it does not require the expert painting techniques of the slow drying oil mediums used by professional portrait painters.

The background, up against the light side of the face, is painted with Viridian in long strokes alternating with Rose Madder, pre-mixed with some Flake White. The color, a shade of gray-green, is related to all parts of the painting and is designed to bring out the glow in the shadows of the face. The same color runs into the shadow between the shirt and the neck.

Here a reminder is in order. All shadows must be kept light from the very start; it is better to have them too light than too dark. If they are kept transparent and light, they will retain their fresh clear color-tone to the end. If they start out too dark, the muddy murk in the shadows will remain to mar the finished painting.

In the description of the finishing stage of the general shadow you will find that the background color is used again, set into the shadow as a reflective, semi-transparent light hovering over the shadow. By relating one color to another a color harmony and balanced relationship between light and shadow will be established.

The jacket is painted next in Cobalt Blue mixed with white and Yellow Ochre. The shadow on the shirt collar is a bluer shade of the same color. Being close to the skin, this shadow will contrast as a clear opposite to the warm color values of the neck.

Yellow-white light over the shirt front is loosely painted up to the drawn line of the right edge of the jacket. This is left unfinished in the illustration in order to show this particular stage of development.

Some professional painters prefer to paint beginning with the light tones; others work toward the light tones by beginning with the shadows.

Here, the painting begins with the light areas, and at the same time the shadows are strengthened as the picture develops and becomes clearer.

The color of the skin—the local color in the light—is a light mixture of white, Zinc-Titanium White, Rose Madder, and Yellow Ochre, brightened a trifle with Cadmium Yellow, light.

Long brush strokes are difficult to manage when beginning the painting of form in a figure painting. This difficulty can be greatly reduced by using a medium-size bright and painting with short strokes in criss-cross fashion; it is a good method for the entire painting except the background, where long strokes create a fine contrast in texture.

The local color of the skin is laid flat up to the edge of the shadow indicating the light.

The same color with Cadmium Red added and some white to vary the shade is used in painting the ear. Sienna and additional red are drawn into the shadow inside the ear.

The face is now beginning to take form and show a likeness. Checking the painting with the mirror, for faulty proportions and other mistakes, should become habitual.

The cool, silvery color tone seen shimmering over the human skin can be imitated in painting by an overlay of a cooler shade of the local color mixed with Crimson.

Criss-crossed in the manner described before, the two shades—the warmer lighter underneath painted first and the cooler on top—set up a simultaneous contrast. As you already know, this means that the two colors are contrasted in such a way as to produce the illusion of a third color which takes place on the retina of the eyes.

Contrast is of the greatest importance in contemporary coloristic painting. The student will have taken a long step toward mastering colorism when he has learned to observe the effect of color contrasts and understand simultaneous contrast.

The cooler local color used as the overlay, made even cooler by adding a little Ultramarine Blue and white, serves as a transition or passage color and is run along the edge and slightly over the shadow. It is not run too far into the shadow color and is not painted as a broad contour, but handled loosely in semi-transparency.

The passage in figure painting builds form quickly and realistically with less effort than any

other method known, but if painted as an even, second edge, it defeats the purpose entirely. Transition tones should be handled like a soft, grayish light floating along the shadow edges.

Before painting the passages, the shadow is strengthened with a darker shade of Burnt Sienna and Cadmium Yellow, deep. Soft sable-hair brights are the best brushes for laying delicate transparency over shadows.

Reflected light between the deepest shadow and the ear is painted in variations of red—orange-red in the tone down the neck and a cooler red close to the ear. Where a still colder color seems to be present, blue and Crimson with white added preserve the colder effect without clashing with nearby colors.

The color of the hair is deepened with Crimson, Ultramarine Blue, and Sienna, and the eyes, pupil, and contour around the iris are also given depth with the same colors.

The background color in transparent values is used as a dark reflected tone in the shadow of the nose, at the side of the head, and on the cheek. Deflected orange light is placed underneath the cheek and further back on the neck.

This brings the painting up to the point shown in the above illustration. Of course, necessary adjustments are made at every stage of the work. A great many mistakes can be avoided by stubbornly adhering to flat painting which, in fact, creates a stronger, more effective color than the rounding off of volume in the building of form. Flat painting of the forms from the beginning will counteract tendencies toward overmodeling.

Symmetry and balance in the color planes and in the light and shadow are achieved by the distribution of the cold and warm color values.

The head, in this exercise, is almost life-size—10 inches from the chin to the top.

PAINTER IN LAMP LIGHT

Two shadows, the darkest values in the color scheme, are the dominating features in this painting. The two shadows contrast with equal strength against the yellow lamp light which envelops the figure and asserts its influence in every part of the painting.

The face shows a strong side light from the right, throwing an equally strong shadow over the features. This light, an intense yellow made of white, Cadmium Yellow, light, and Rose Madder, had to be strong enough to be in direct contrast to the purple shadow behind the face,

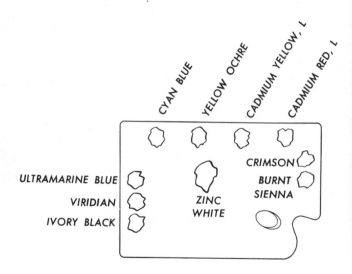

and to the black in front. Rose Madder, painted directly into the wet yellow, modeled the face in half-shadows on the light side of the face; in the shadows, to the left, it was used as half light, with deep shadows in a purple made of white, Cyan Blue and Crimson. A similar mixture in the shadow behind the face brought the face out in full contrast.

The flat form of the black shadow over the green sweater brought the lower part of the painting into strong focus. The light tone is white, Viridian, some Ultramarine Blue and Yellow Ochre, scraped to represent woolen texture. This acts as a third milder contrast.

Light Cyan Blue in the shirt is reflected upwards on the left jaw; this small cool spot of color is necessary to the entire combination of colors in the painting.

Black was painted into the rose and purple shadows of the face, as the deepest depth, bringing the modeling up to full plastic form.

Touches of white in the eyes, and the lips painted in rose, mixed from Cadmium Red and white, finished the features and unified the colors in the face.

White and Sienna modeled the hair, which was topped with a black beret. A weak highlight of purple over the hair and in the black, rounded the head. On each side of the purple shadow, shadowy forms were painted into fresh yellow, wet in wet, with rose and the purple combined in warmer and cooler contrasts. In this way, a quieting effect was achieved.

A Sienna-brown palette, and a yellow and a rose-red brush with brown handles—the brushes pointing at a bright yellow spot in the light—furnished a stable foundation for the picture.

This painting was limited to a few bright shades of color contrasted against dark strong forms. Such paintings of subjects in artificial light are good exercises in the control of strong contrasts.

WESTERN FRESCO PAINTER

The cool effect of the light from daylight lamps on the local colors, the colors of the objects themselves, is interesting as a separate painting problem and is demonstrated in this exercise.

In this particular kind of painting, cold and warm grays play an important role in balancing and quieting the color scheme. The #2 painting medium is employed as a thinner and sparingly used in alla prima painting.

In the picture, the wet, fresh plaster coating is flooded with cool light; the figure is in the colder, bluer shadow. Warmer shadows, in contrast, are produced simultaneously in the hat, the folds of the shirt, and the pants.

The figure was drawn in warm Ochre-Sienna, with Venetian Red added to the color of the head. Blue was added to the elbows and the same blue was used in the enamel-plate palette. Cobalt Blue over the hat, shirt, and pants finished the general light tonality over the figure.

Black hair with a Cobalt highlight, rose-gray flesh shadows, gray shoes, and a blue edge around the palette placed the figure in direct relationship to the black in the background.

On the plaster the wavy lines in black and Venetian Red, and the black and Sienna heads indicate the beginning of the fresco. Underneath, the outline of a sheep is seen, ready for the underpainting in fresco to follow.

To the right, an uncovered area of the darker, coarser fresco ground shows. This is painted in a gray tone made from Cobalt, Cadmium Red, and white-gray. Texture is scraped into the wet color with the palette knife to imitate the texture of the coarser plaster undercoating.

Against this gray, there is a brown plank holding a fresco painter's paint box with pots and brushes in bright colors, and a long hand rest. This group is also bathed in the cold light, the cool blue holding the color scheme together.

On the other side of the figure are three more paint pots. These are smeared by yellow, blue, and gray paint.

On the right side, the rough red-gray plaster area is a shade warmer and darker. This value corresponds to the cooler shadow over the wall in the lower left corner. Balancing one cool

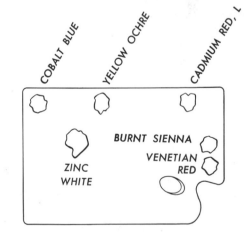

gray against another, near each other in value, tends to quiet strong dominating forms in decorative patterns.

The Sienna shadow, on the side of the paint box, keeps the warm tones in the gray color from looking muddy because the simultaneous contrast set up by the Sienna results in a cooler gray. At the top of the wall, the Venetian Red lines have the same effect on the gray.

ST. CHRISTOPHER OF CANYON DE CHELLY

During my first visit to Canyon de Chelly a thunderstorm came up over the canyon. The scene before me, illuminated by lightning in sharply contrasted coloring, had grandeur.

As usual, I drew a quick, simplified sketch, and indicated the local colors on the drawing. My brief notes describing the different effects of the illumination of the lightning on the local colors were immensely helpful later when I painted this picture.

I saw a Navajo man walking over the rain-swollen stream on the canyon floor, carrying a child on his shoulder. Feeling his way with a stick, he walked beside me under an overhanging cliff.

The scene struck me as a ready-made composition for Saint Christopher carrying the Christ Child over the stream.

Cadmium Red. Additional strokes of Ultramarine and Crimson in these forms deepen the darkness into a solid black.

A forked discharge of lightning flashing across the sky is painted Cadmium Yellow with an edging of Ultramarine Blue on each side. This blue, barely discernible, is a darker tone than the yellow.

Both sides of the picture show the typical shelves and overhangs of the Venetian Red cliffs and the precipitous canyon walls.

Reflections in the water behind the figure are painted pure white, blue, and violet.

Icy blue-greens in darker values, Yellow Ochre, and purplish grays are found in the middle distance and in the foreground.

The Child is painted in shades of soft violet, gray, and white. The halo is dark yellow and blue.

A gunny sack thrown over the man's head is shaded in brown-violet with darker shadows

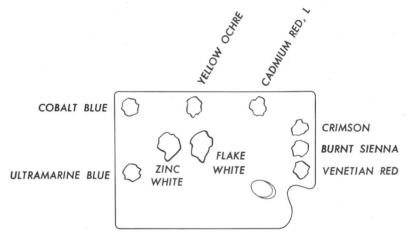

Canyon de Chelly, with its somber red walls and gloomy atmosphere, left a melancholy impression on my mind, seeing it as I did on a murky day. Knowing its history of brutality only strengthened my impression.

The color in the picture is built entirely upon a flash of lightning. The thundercloud almost hidden behind gray sheets of rain is painted in a gray made by mixing Venetian Red, Cobalt Blue, and white.

The darker shadings have more of the blue, and brush strokes of Cadmium Red are drawn in.

The black silhouetted clouds at the upper left corner are painted in pure Cobalt Blue and

in Sienna modeling.

His Cobalt Blue tunic, with white highlights and Ultramarine Blue shadows, has effective reflected light in Yellow Ochre with Sienna deeper in the folds.

The face is in dark browns with shining, wet highlights of blue and blue-white. Arms and legs in middle tones of Yellow Ochre and Sienna have dark blue-violet shadows and still deeper accents of Sienna.

Scintillating spots of light on the wet cliffs are scraped up with the palette knife. This is an example showing how vibrating color—the old Italian masters' *vibrato*—is used to create illuminated, wet, rough planes.

Chapter 8

Landscape Problems

In the first two books of this series we took up landscapes—very simple ones in the first book, and more complicated ones in the second.

In this, the third book, we have explored the beginning of portrait painting at some length. You will notice that we still paint, in most cases, with essentially the same palette, although our color emphasis varies from painting to painting.

In the following section we will discuss some landscape paintings which, though still simple, are more complicated than those found in the previous books. By this time, the student should have enough skill and experience to enable him to duplicate these exercises with a degree of craftsmanship.

COOL WATER

Early summer-morning light floods the scene, gilding the trees and bushes in the foreground. The lifting mist silvers the birches in the background.

The deep blue in the zenith is reflected in the pool. The dark bottom of the pool converts this sky-blue into a dominant of a darker, deeper blue. Because of this dominating blue, the surrounding colors were put in with variations of strong colors opposed to the blue. Only near complementaries are needed to activate and harmonize the tonality.

Even the strongly emphasized big trunk of the old oak is not strong enough to take command over the blue pool. In the right relationship, strong volume and strong color seem to check and balance each other.

Against the warm, pinkish blue-gray sky, the birches in the lingering mist look gray-green, warmed with ochre. The evergreens are in warm light and blue-green shadows, with still deeper depths set in with loosely mixed Crimson and Sienna.

The building to the right, in a light color on the sunny side, has a gray roof, a lighter gray shadow on the shady side, orange in the shade of

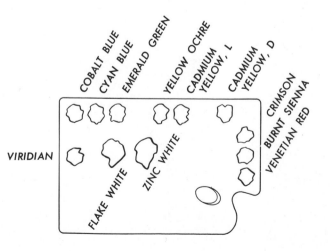

the eaves, and a blue shadow below on the wall. Warm pinkish-gray in the road and on the house serves as a convenient interval between the background and stronger foreground greens.

Foliage, at the top, is lit by the morning sunshine, golden and bright. This was begun by painting in flat masses in transparency, using Permanent Emerald Green with Cadmium Yellow, light, and some white. Green-blue shadows were painted in the hanging forms of the green leaves. Ochre and Sienna in darker and lighter mixtures with Cadmium Yellow, deep, painted between and in front of this cool green, create a bright distinct color tone that harmonizes the foliage into a strong opposite to the blue mirror-pool.

Middle-ground grass and bushes, painted in the same color scheme, have colder blue overtones to the right, and deep blue and Crimson in the shadows. Toward the opposite edge, greens are more yellow-brown in tone.

Half-light over the big oak trunk was first painted in Cobalt Blue, rose, and Ochre. This was scraped down to a thin coat of gray, then the bark was laid over with Venetian Red and white, with blue highlighting finished in palette-knife painting. Final modeling of the bark was done in deep purple, with orange reflected light and details in Sienna and Viridian. Darker shades of the same colors made the wavy mirror reflections in the pool. The deep blue itself, made of Ultramarine and Cyan Blue, was reinforced in the deepest depths with Crimson, Viridian, Sienna, and blue, sinking almost to black in some places.

Extremely faint shades of Cobalt Blue set into these different darks, especially on the right bank over the water and the bushes above, correlate the middle distance and the foreground trees. The tree trunks, in silhouetted shadow to the left and one to the right, were painted in deep brown, made of Viridian and Sienna. The trunk of the tree, to the left in the foreground, was lighted with orange. On the right-hand side a smaller tree in deep purple, with the lower part warmed by Sienna, repeats its coloring in wavy reflections in the water. A few brighter whirls reflected from the sunlit bushes above were painted into the dark reflections.

Finally, a spot of grass in full sunlight tied the two sides of the pool together in the general tonality of the scene.

This painting is reproduced in color on the color spread.

RED BARN, SUNLIT ROAD

This sunlit road running through a wooded dell is painted from one of my water colors; it is one of the many scenes I learned to love in the farm country of Dutchess County.

The red barn as color contrast strengthens the cold and warm painting of the trees and bushes. The light-gray boarded partition and the light-pinkish road make a pair of passage tones between the red barn and the shadowy part of the verdure, which is painted in Viridian, Ultramarine Blue, Ochre, Sienna, and deeper notes of Rose Madder and blue.

Sunlit branches in yellow-greens—Permanent Emerald Green and Cadmium Yellows—are warmed up in reflected light with Ochre and Sienna shades.

Intermediary shadows deeper in the background are painted in blue or warmer, greener variations of the general color scheme. A series of vertical intervals of cold and warm color runs over the leafy branches in the background.

The red of the barn—Cadmium Red and Sienna—has an atmospheric sheen of cold Crimson with some white glazed over the boards. From the road a color-echo over the shiny tin roof completes the color orbit.

Note the modeling of the masses indi-

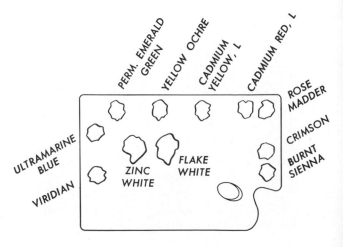

cating leafy branches in strong sunlight. There is form with a feeling of transparency.

Strong sunlight produces deep shadows. Leaves on trees can form either opaque masses, or semi-transparent screens which filter the sunlight, depending on the direction of the light. If the tree is seen against the sunlight, the sky is reflected on top of the leaves and the lower branches receive reflections from the ground. If the tree is lighted by direct light, then the forms tend to flatten out and in strong direct sunlight, to decolorize.

Light can be captured in a picture only by constantly observing and painting its behavior.

THUNDERSTORM

Here is a picture painted from a sketch I made in one of the western plains states.

At the upper left corner there is a greenish-blue patch of sky. The rest of the sky is covered by a misty gray, which starts at the left as a blue green-gray and ends at the right in a pink-gray. At the horizon, light pink-yellow clouds disappear into the mist.

In the far distance, above and below the big dark cloud in the middle distance, thunderheads are shaded in a rosy pinkish-gray made of Rose Madder, white, and Cadmium Red, with Yellow Ochre reflected into it.

The typical shining highlights on the top edges of the cloud formations are painted in opaque white with heavy half-white, made of equal parts of Zinc White and Titanium White. This white was employed throughout the picture. Only Medium #1 was used.

The great copper-colored cloud in the middle distance is painted in semi-opaque coloring with some slightly transparent places.

Cloud formations in turmoil are seen moving upwards in great sweeps, driven by gusts of strong winds. Shadings in copper color made of white, Venetian Red, and Ochre, combined with soft lines drawn in Venetian Red, are used as form-building values.

A dark edge of a cloud in the center and the dark thunderhead higher up to the extreme left are colored blue and blended with the red to form a dark purple. The edges of these clouds are outlined in a golden tone of Cadmium Yellow, light.

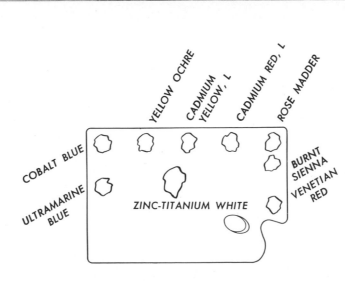

COBALT BLUE

ULTRAMARINE BLUE

YELLOW OCHRE

CADMIUM YELLOW, L

CADMIUM RED, L

ROSE MADDER

BURNT SIENNA

VENETIAN RED

ZINC-TITANIUM WHITE

The rainstorm is painted in the same color scheme as the clouds but darkened to a blue-black gray. The left half of the rain is scratched in with the palette knife. A bluer, darker cloud shadow is moving over the ground. Similar blue shadows sharpen the horizon line, contrasting with the vague greens in the ochre-colored landscape.

Foreground grass in full light is painted a gray-green at the top, with strokes of Ochre and Cadmium Yellow, light, lower down.

Finally, the first stroke of lightning, the so-called "leader," was underpainted in Ultramarine Blue mixed with white. This was allowed to dry for a few days before the lightning itself could be painted. Sharp Cadmium Yellow, light, and white were set off in heavy opaque color to cut a clean brilliant line over the blue underpainting.

Rainstorms, storm clouds, and thick misty skies are always painted with mixtures of the three iron oxides—Venetian Red, Light Red, or the heavier Indian Red—in combinations with Cobalt Blue and white, warmed by adding Yellow Ochre or black.

All such color schemes can easily be made to work, as either cold or warm values in rain or storm skies, by adding more of the blue for cold and more red for warmer and deeper shades. They can be changed at will, one way or the other, and enriched by additional tones of Yellow Ochre or Cadmium Yellow and Sienna broken to a low-colored orange. Together they produce the tones of copper color, common in stormy weather, particularly thunderstorm cloud formations.

Fifteen years ago I had a wonderful opportunity to watch and paint an enormous thundercloud looming on the horizon 70 miles away. At dusk this cloud turned into a tornado, which fortunately moved away. I watched this cloud, illuminated in brilliant colors by inner lightning, moving and disappearing over the Oklahoma horizon at nightfall; it was an awesome spectacle, like a giant top in the sky slowly beginning to spin, then turning faster and faster.

THE STYLIZED LANDSCAPE

The mountain ranges in this stylized landscape are painted from realistic sketches made
in high altitude regions such as the pen and ink
sketch above. The reflective power of the snow
brings about surprising changes, revising or dis-
torting patterns of color and form. Moving
clouds break up and create new contrasts. Entirely new situations occur in the landscape.
Many quick sketches in crayon, and color
notations are the best means for recording the
rapid changes of light.

In this painting, strong opposites in dark
and light run through hues of blue-black, purple-
black, and green-black.

The glistening snow-covered peaks in the
background provide relief from the harsh black
and brown cliffs in the foreground.

The stylization evident in this landscape
lies in the simplification of form and color. The
outlines of the forms are simplified into smooth
curves.

Jutting out in the center is the dark stone
wall of a cliff. The darkest color of the cliff is
painted in the complementary black of Rose
Madder and viridian in shades ranging from
gray-black to greenish black.

Lighter, warm shades in the black are
introduced by painting and blending with Yellow Ochre.

On the rock shelf in the middle, a greenish-
blue snow patch lies in the shadow. Blueish-
white snow covers the top of the cliff. Stained
snow, over and under the shelf, is painted red-
gray in semi-transparent hues. Lighter forma-

tions are painted in a warm green-gray.

Two groups of stunted trees were first painted white; later after drying, they were glazed over in green-blue and the highlights wiped off with a rag. A gray stone shelf on a steep rock wall is partly covered with light-blue snow. The same blue runs all the way under the cliff in the center.

On the right, a sheer precipice in shadings of black and crimson cuts off the view. Another steep wall on the left is painted in black-green, viridian and Rose Madder.

The main variations of the stone color are made from blue and ochre. Darker spots have Cyan Blue and Cadmium Red enriching the color of the dark stone walls.

Forms of green-gray, lower down, are high-altitude flora, moss, and so forth.

The blue-gray color used for the snow form clinging to the the wall also covers the foot of the hill, and is used in spotty shadings on the trail bending around the cliff. The same color is found in the snow over the foreground; red and green rock is blown free of snow further down.

To the left, standing against the yellow-green sky, a blue-black mountain peak is shaded down to a lighter gray. Two forms in a lighter, warmer gray indicate ice and snow-covered rock formations.

The snowfield curving downward has dazzling whites in green and blue hues in the ridges and drifts.

On the right side another higher peak with two sunlit snow fields towers in the sky. This sunlit pyramid in white, with Cadmium Yellow, has blue-violet snow shadows all the way down to the sunny snow field below. Lower, the shadows change to a lighter gray with two dark gray shadows shaped in the form of crescents. In other places there are sharply pointed long shadows in gray-blue.

Blue-gray snow clouds are sailing over the mountains, against a sky of yellow-green made of Permanent Emerald Green, white, and Cadmium Yellow, light. Red and Cobalt Blue, in darker and lighter hues of gray, are painted into the cloud forms at the top. A long cloud formation hangs down over the left peak, in light coloring of white-yellow in the light, and gray-violet in the shadow. Further over to the right, the clouds change into light pink, the shadows into a warmer pink, and finally disappear into the mist.

Paintings that are rich in detail of color forms such as this one, invariably take their cue from two constants; in this case from the dark cliffs in the foreground, and the whitest value of the snow. By painting these two extremes first, valuable leads toward the other tones will follow.

Once balance and control of the values are established, color and form should fall into place everywhere in the painting.

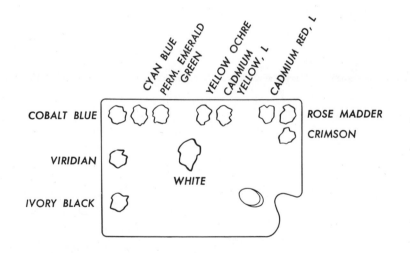

SUNSET

The fear of being regarded as a naive sentimentalist keeps many artists from trying their hand at painting a sunrise, a sunset, or moonlight—all extremely good exercises in colorism.

The elusive culmination point in the light of the rising or setting sun, and the somewhat difficult light over the moonlit landscape should be a welcome challenge to any painter.

A back street in a Hudson River town served as the subject for this sunset picture. It had all the helpful features of light gray passages and green intervals that I have written about earlier in describing other pictures.

Against the warm grass-green at the bottom, there is a warm light-gray with cold shadows in the middle distance which is broken only by the white-gray building to the right. The small pines help to break the monotony of the large area of gray. By painting the pine on the edge of the grass in a bluer green, the foreground shadow was kept intact as a color unit.

This painting was done with my back to the sunset, facing the eastern sky. The glow from the sunset was reflected in bands of color. I painted what I saw. At the top of the painting there is a light transparency of Ultramarine Blue premixed with white, with the edge thinned out with Rose Madder to form a lighter passage into a broader band of Viridian Green; all this is done in transparent painting. Below is a narrow orange cloud that has broken loose from the green color above. A white top edge contrasts with both the green above and the heavy atmosphere below. White, Rose Madder and some Cadmium Red render the dense atmosphere seen in the lower sky over the horizon after a hot day.

The mountains and the distant forest are painted in modeling strokes with Ultramarine Blue, broken into a grayer shade with rose and Ochre in the lighter places. There is a darker gray in the church tower reaching into the sky. Sunlit trees in front of the blue forest are gilded by the last rays of the sun.

Such light effects change quickly and must be rapidly painted. A separate brush for each color used is a must.

Cadmium Yellow and Viridian are loosely mixed into a light yellow-green for the light; Permanent Emerald Green, in a similar mixture with the same yellow in the deeper shade, is used for the shadow.

These colors are picked up on the brushes in thick lumps and set off directly on the canvas without palette mixing. The lights and shadows are painted in rapid succession with a minimum of brush work and followed with lighter and deeper purple-blue to indicate individual trees. The same purple, made deeper with blue-green, rose, and orange, is also used in the darker shadows. Higher up to the extreme right, tall pines are painted in the same shadow colors. Below the pines, in sharp contrast, is a light green tree highlighted in the Cadmium yellows, with deep shadows in Ochre and Sienna, and

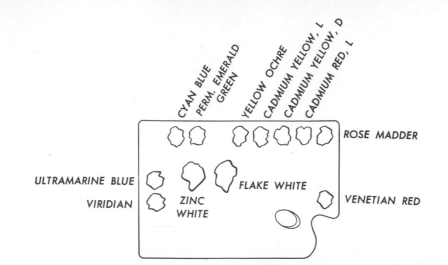

CYAN BLUE
PERM. EMERALD GREEN
YELLOW OCHRE
CADMIUM YELLOW, L
CADMIUM YELLOW, D
CADMIUM RED, L

ROSE MADDER

ULTRAMARINE BLUE

VIRIDIAN

ZINC WHITE

FLAKE WHITE

VENETIAN RED

cold violet optic light.

Into this color scheme of golden light, the clear blue color of a roof is placed in the cold shadow to intensify the glow.

A high maple stands far out to the left, painted in a half-light tone made of Permanent Emerald Green, Ochre, and some white with Cyan blue-green in the shadow.

The small bushes growing in front of the white building, the trees on both sides and in the background serve to frame the cluster of houses.

The highest buildings are bathed in Cadmium Yellow, light, their shadow turned blueish in simultaneous contrast to the strong yellow. Light and shadow are automatically balanced without loss of light or color. The older houses in lower values of local colors are also intensified in the same way, one with a deep blue roof, another with a rust-colored roof and two white dormer windows.

Toward the left, a smaller house half in shadow is white with a blue sheen glazed over it. Next to the left, the two-storied brick building, roofed in warm black-gray, effectively brings out the lighter warmer colors of the other houses. Venetian Red, Sienna, and white, scraped lengthwise over the light side of the bricks, make a harmonious shade of brick red. Rose and blue added to the red make a mildly contrasting shadow. Light ochre-colored window trims and darker half-drawn shades stand out against the blue-green black window panes; along with the brown door they are accents of value to the general tonality.

An old dilapidated frame building stands where the street turns to the right. Originally an ochre color, the paint is flaking off showing the gray-blue of the weathered boards.

The color is influenced by the nearby sources of light and color and gets reflections of both light and color from every side. The tones seem to shift from warm to cold.

To "antique" the old structure, I painted the siding in light Ochre and pulled the color off with the palette knife. A mixture of white, Cyan Blue and Ochre was laid loosely over the scraped undercoating. This, too, was lightly scraped with the knife which exposed the light yellow in spots and produced the effect of flaked-off paint. Board joints were outlined in weak gray-purple. Deeper shadows of Crimson warmed with Sienna, dark door openings, the broken window, and the shadow under the eaves, completed the walls. The rust-colored sheet-iron roof, blackened at the top, the lighter dormer roof, hanging doors and sagging trims were all illuminated and gilded by the setting sun.

Bushes were painted in warm greens with optic light over the top branches. Two blue-gray garbage cans placed under the bushes united the green colors on both sides of the picture.

This painting is reproduced in full color on the color spread.

AUTUMN LANDSCAPE

In this painting slightly calligraphic brush drawing in color varies the form-building of the trees.

The gray-green passage tone of the middle distant grass and the yellow-brown band at the bottom of the tall grass on the low-lying ground contrast with the reds, purples, and greens in the autumn coloring of the leaves.

Bright golden hues, orange shades of Cadmium, light, and dark yellow with Burnt Sienna are separated from the cool reds and pinks by dark green trees. These dark shades of green are Viridian and Ultramarine Blue with Crimson, warmed here and there by deepening tones of Ochre and orange.

Brush strokes of light blue over the tree tops soften the silhouette with optic light. Patches of green grass under the trees, and the rose-gray sheen of dry grass over the middle plane bring the color lanes together in the cool airiness of an autumn day.

In this picture we see that the element of decoration does not necessarily turn a picture into a piece of decorative art; skill and restraint can prevent the painting from becoming a mere formal ornamental panel.

Although the much-abused conventionalized decorative representations have created a distaste for all forms of decoration in painting, enrichment of the color scheme by discreet use of ornamentation should not be overlooked merely because it has been overdone in the past.

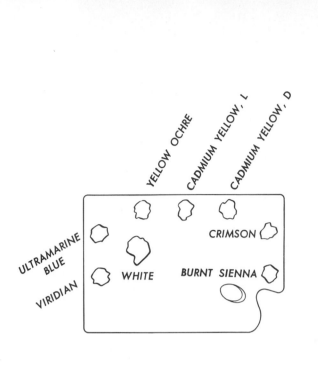

ULTRAMARINE BLUE
VIRIDIAN
YELLOW OCHRE
CADMIUM YELLOW, L
CADMIUM YELLOW, D
CRIMSON
WHITE
BURNT SIENNA

NOVEMBER FOG

Diffused light, filtering through the fog-shroud over a landscape, may constitute a formidable color problem. The error of thinking that fog is merely a gray substance floating about becomes painfully clear the first time one tries to paint such a scene direct from nature.

The lifting fog, especially when a glimmer of the sun comes through, however faint, immediately lets loose the whole array of spectrum colors. Coloring in black and white only will certainly not depict the elusive quality of the moving fog with its endlessly shifting tonality. Sudden light over an object, seen through a rent in the gray wall, disrupts the color scheme in that spot immediately.

This is exactly what happened to the group of trees in the middle distance to the right in my painting. I first started painting in flat masses. Suddenly the trees became alive with light, shadows, and depth, all against a blue patch of sky and the golden colors of the early morning sun shining behind the low branches near the base.

The sky, in shimmering Ultramarine Blue, had to be tied in with the larger portion of the landscape, still in the thick, gray fog. In order to do so, the gray-producing complementary colors—Cobalt Blue and Cadmium Red, light, warmed up and controlled by adding Yellow Ochre and Ivory Black—changed the sky into a more colorful gray.

The painting was begun with a light outlining of the houses in charcoal. Then, beginning at the left side, the gray was painted in over the entire background. Painted into this gray color, the smaller house was shaded entirely in Venetian

Red-blue and the roof was done in lighter blue-gray made from the same colors broken a trifle with black.

Next, the same colors, in a stronger shade of red, were painted over the walls and the chimneys of the larger house. The roof, equal in color value to the walls, had blue and black added to make the color a colder shade of gray. The window shades and window frames were painted a light yellow made of Yellow Ochre. Dark gray shadows inside the frames and a line of Sienna indicating the sloping roof-gutter were finishing touches on the house.

The thinner edge of the fog to the right has white and a barely discernible Cadmium Yellow and Rose Madder painted into the gray mist to show the faint light shining through. Autumn-colored branches painted against the blue sky vary in rose-gray and a darker purple-gray. Darker shadows deepened with Sienna have the same softly focused values.

A short distance behind the taller trees, bushes lit up by the early sun were painted in bright golden oranges and browns made of Sienna broken with Cadmium Yellow, deep, Rose

Madder, and Ochre. Purple-blue branches hanging in front—another set of stronger complementaries—are used to contrast with the orange colors beyond, thus enhancing their brightness.

The grayish-white wall partition and the brown-gray weeds in front change to a colder blue at the right end, and also receive some of the gold seen above the wall.

The cement walk, in a warmer gray that is still warmer in the shadow of the edge of the walk, is made to contrast with the colder color of the railroad bed. The bluish-gray of the steel is done in black and white with cold white highlights.

To outline the rails, I used a beveled straightedge—handled, as I have explained before, bevel down with one end of the straightedge held up to keep it off the wet surface underneath. A flat, thin bristle brush is held lightly with the index finger and the thumb, and run along the edge of the bevel.

The slightly transparent Zinc White, employed with all the colors and thinned with Medium #2, made it possible to paint in semi-transparency over the semi-opaque color coats.

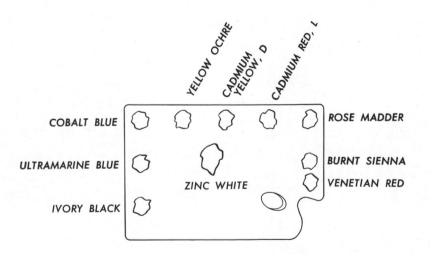

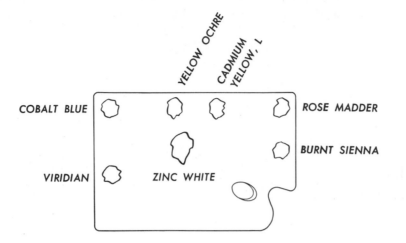

COBALT BLUE   YELLOW OCHRE   CADMIUM YELLOW, L   ROSE MADDER

BURNT SIENNA

VIRIDIAN   ZINC WHITE

LANDSCAPE IN THE STYLE OF THE ROMANTIC ERA

From the time of the Barbizon school of French painters, we have had followers of what could be called the "romantic" school of painting. Whether these romantics did settings for romantic operas or genre painting for the salon, they always painted representations of their personal feelings. Their favorite subjects were landscapes, street scenes, interiors, animals, and groups of people laughing or crying or just sitting around.

By way of Corot and others, Claude Lorrain's style of silhouetted forms and tonal values of simplified light and shadow found its way into the canvases of the romantics and the "illuminarists."

Here, in my own painting, I have endeavored to catch the style of painting the silhouetted form that was prevalent in the romantic era. Mistakenly, these paintings are sometimes called "primitives" which is an entirely different kind of painting done by an entirely different kind of painter.

My first contact with this particular manner of composing a landscape came about in my early childhood when I started copying the landscapes printed on the window shades in my home.

The painting reproduced here derives partly from the window shade decor, and partly from memories of romantic painters' work. Oddly enough, it is quite modern in feeling and should give the beginner a clear idea of the simplified form with sharp contrasts of light and shadow.

In this example, underpainting begins by painting the sky, the lightest parts of the water, and the foreground in the same light yellow tone. The mountain, bushes, and trees are underpainted in Cobalt Blue; the house, the tree trunks, and branches, in Rose Madder.

The blacks used are complementary mixtures of Viridian and Sienna or Rose Madder. The turpentine-thinned colors in the undercoatings set quickly and can be followed by colors thinned moderately with oil-turpentine medium.

The silhouettes are placed in juxtaposition in cold and warm color. Viridian and Ultramarine Blue are used mainly in the cold tonalities, and warmed with Ochre and Sienna in the warmer values.

Additional depth in forms and shadows is achieved by accenting with Rose Madder and blue, or Sienna. Yellow Ochre added to the greens warms or softens the verdure.

Light added here and there over the leafy edges of the trees and over the foreground grass completes this greeting from a bygone era.

The student should remember that descriptions of this kind are only meant to serve as guides to procedure. It would be impossible, of course, to go into every brush stroke in detail, although there are many more things I would like to tell you. For example, touches of deep blue and Crimson reinforced with Sienna help to bring branches of greens forward; bright spots of yellow-green can be set in around the tree roots to contrast with these deeper, colder touches of color. But such uses of small areas of color, and other matters, become too involved for detailed explanation. They are among the things that each painter must observe and work out in his own way.

This completes the specific instruction part of the *Course In Beginning Oil Painting*. If you have diligently followed the instructions and practiced the exercises, you should now be able to paint pleasing pictures of subjects of your own choosing.

Book 4, a *Handbook* concerned largely with materials, is a valuable reference work. However, it also contains a group of examples and exercises that are carefully planned to serve as refresher practice in technique.

Handbook
of Methods
and Materials for
Course in Beginning
OIL PAINTING

Olle Nordmark

Introduction

This *Handbook* is the fourth volume of the series, *Course in Beginning Oil Painting*. Although some painting techniques will be discussed, and more advanced painting exercises given, it has been planned to serve as a reference manual for the materials of oil painting and their correct use and preparation.

Oil painting is painting with color pigments ground in fatty oils which dry when exposed to air.

The durability of the painting depends upon the ability of the oils to absorb oxygen from the air and harden into transparent surfaces. The oils are the binders and protectors of the color pigments. When the process of absorption has come to an end, the painting is said to have dried.

Durability of the color pigments, processed into powders, depends upon the quality of the raw material. Endless tests of various kinds must be constantly made with the oil and the pigments themselves. Answers must be found to the differences in behavior of the materials under different conditions. There are many problems connected with the manufacturing of the materials as well as with their use in the actual painting of a picture. All such problems must be solved before the materials are milled, mixed and packaged.

Two kinds of painting surfaces are in general use—canvas and panel materials. In both, excellence of quality is of the utmost importance to the painting. Of equal importance are the priming materials used to make up the foundation that carries the colors. The sequence of building up such a foundation must be followed with the utmost care.

The tools for applying the colors over the priming are brushes and painting knives.

Mixing and conditioning of the colors is done on a palette with brushes or a palette knife.

For conditioning—making the colors thinner, leaner, or fatter—various painting mediums must be compounded. Only three mediums are needed for most methods of oil painting; each has a different influence on the colors.

The thinner used in the three mediums is the all-important gum turpentine. Turpentine can also be employed by itself as a thinner under certain conditions.

Driers, sometimes used in mediums to hasten the drying of the color film, are risky components and are excluded entirely in the methods I suggest.

Retouching varnish is essential; it is rubbed over absorbent mat areas in the color surface before the overpainting begins.

When a painting is finished and completely dry, it needs an extra overlay of picture varnish—a final varnish to protect the colors from deterioration caused by impurities in the air.

These are the main topics that will be explored here. It is my hope that the student will use this Handbook in conjunction with the other three books; thus increasing his knowledge of materials and their use at the same time that he is developing his skill and understanding of the principles of oil painting.

Olle Nordmark

Chapter 1

Painting Surfaces

Linen canvas is the most commonly used surface for oil painting. For hundreds of years artists have used it, in all kinds of weaves and qualities, and it is still by far the most satisfactory. Only the tightly woven kind should be used for self-prepared canvas. It is easier to size and prime than the loosely woven variety.

Cotton canvas is also frequently used, because it is less expensive than linen. It is a good substitute for linen canvas for the beginner, although it is not as durable, nor does it have as satisfactory a "feel" to the professional. It should not be used for stretcher-mounted paintings larger than 30 inches in either dimension as it is likely to have too much "give." It is made in a variety of weaves, but only the heavier ones are suitable for painting, such as duck, sailcloth, and heavy sheeting. Sailcloth is woven with one side twilled and the other smooth. I find the twilled side very pleasant to paint on. For a smoother surface, the other side can be used.

Linen, medium fine

Linen, fine

Linen, twill

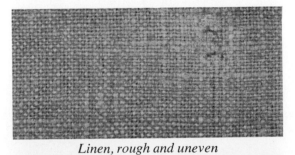

Linen, rough and uneven

Cotton, sailcloth

Linen, medium texture

Masonite board—section on right has been primed with white lead.

Tempered Masonite Board, a modern building material, is an excellent painting surface. One side is very smooth, and the other textured during its manufacture by the imprint of a screen, like window screening. Either side can be prepared for painting. This material is widely used by contemporary painters.

Thin Masonite panels are particularly well suited for outdoor work. Several panels can be carried, wet, in a grooved carrying frame with perfect safety.

Canvas panels, made of good quality cotton canvas, primed and sized, and mounted on stiff cardboard, have been on the market for quite some time. This is a very popular, ready-to-paint surface, which is very satisfactory for smaller paintings.

Some cheaper panels are made with paper instead of cotton canvas. The paper is embossed to simulate canvas, and treated to receive the paint.

Linen canvas panels are also available, costing about twice the price of the cotton canvas ones.

These prepared panels can also be carried in grooved carrying cases, or held apart with double-ended canvas pins. These pins are also used to separate wet stretcher-mounted canvases, but cannot be used with Masonite due to its hardness.

Oil painting paper is available in sheets, usually 18 by 23 inches. It has a canvas-like texture and is primed to give it a grain very similar to canvas. It is an economical and satisfactory canvas substitute for students and for practice painting.

STRETCHING THE CANVAS.

Canvas must be supported to permit the application of paint. This is done by mounting it on a frame called a stretcher. The stretcher is made of four wooden stretcher strips, shaped and mitered at the corners so that they will form a frame when pushed together. These strips are available at art stores in sizes from 8 to 60 inches long. A well equipped store will have them in every inch size within this range. Special sizes can be made on request in most art stores.

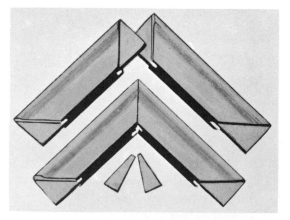

Stretcher strips for canvas

To make a stretcher, two pairs of strips are assembled. The combinations of length and width are almost endless when you consider the variety of sizes available. Small wooden wedges are inserted in the slots provided in the inner corners, to stretch the canvas.

Unprepared canvas can be stretched on the stretcher without using the stretching tongs which are necessary for stretching prepared canvas. These tongs, or pliers, are a combination of tack hammer and plier, and cost between three and four dollars.

When unprepared canvas is mounted on the stretcher and sized, it will shrink taut.

The corners of the assembled stretcher strips are hammered tight and checked for squareness with a carpenter's try square, or a drafting triangle.

Place the frame on top of the canvas, and center the frame, allowing 1 inch of canvas for tacking to the sides. Start with a tack in the center of one side, and then place a tack near each corner. The tacks should be driven only

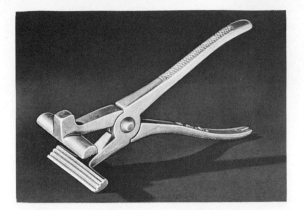

Canvas stretching tongs

Hold the canvas edge with one hand, push a tack in place, and drive it in. Finish all four sides in this way, up to the distance of two tacks from the corners where the canvas edges are tucked in; then finish each side with smaller size tacks to avoid cracking the wood in the corners. Upholsterer's #4 tacks, with flat heads, are commonly used. Space tacks 1½ to 2 inches apart.

SELF-PREPARED PAINTING GROUNDS.

Canvas or panel material used for painting surfaces must first receive two coats of glue size before being primed with white lead. The size stops the suction in the surface and protects it from the raw linseed oil in the primer. Any canvas turns dark and becomes brittle if saturated with oil. Cotton canvas eventually rots. The size coatings are fully protective and prevent deterioration of the canvas.

The Size. To make glue size, two kinds of glue have been used throughout the history of painting: rabbitskin glue and gelatine glue.

The rabbitskin glue is especially valuable for its fine quality. It is sold in cakes or in powder form. Cake glue must first be pounded into small pieces with a hammer, the cake wrapped in a square of strong cloth to prevent the glue from flying about. Do this against a solid support.

One ounce of the glue is placed in a can holding a little more than a pint. The glue is barely covered with cold water and left to soak overnight.

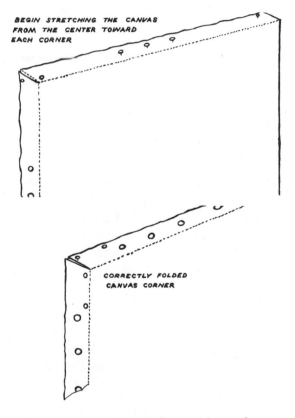

BEGIN STRETCHING THE CANVAS FROM THE CENTER TOWARD EACH CORNER

CORRECTLY FOLDED CANVAS CORNER

about three-quarters of the way in so they can be easily removed for later restretching of the canvas. Stretch the canvas across the frame in the middle, and tack the opposite side. Stretch and tack the remaining two sides, also starting in the middle with one tack. Finish by returning to the first side, stretching from the center towards the corners, 5 or 6 inches at a time.

One pint of water is heated to the boiling point and poured over the softened glue a little at a time, stirring until all the glue is mixed with the water. Place the can in a pot of boiling water, and heat again without bringing the glue to a boil. Boiling spoils the adhesiveness of all glues.

Sizing. Remove the pot from the stove. Place the stretched canvas on a table, protected with newspaper, and begin laying on the first size coat. The sizing is done with an ordinary housepainter's brush, 3 to 4 inches wide. The edges of the canvas are coated first. Begin by laying on a lane of size the width of the brush. Brush crosswise to even out. The brush is held in a slightly slanting position, to produce more of a "laying on" than a "rubbing in" of the size over the weave.

Proceed laying lane after lane, brushing the adjoining edges together, until the whole surface is covered. After the sizing is completed the canvas is left to dry overnight. This first coat is called the "key coat."

Before the application of the second coat, the dry surface is given a light sandpapering with a medium rough sandpaper. Cut the paper in the middle, fold one of the halves, and hold the paper with the fingers spread wide.

Glue size can also be applied cold in a jellied state. Jellied size is poured out in the middle of the canvas and spread towards the sides with a spatula or a drafting triangle.

Finish without stopping, keeping a close watch for poorly covered spots and pinholes, which can be seen by holding the canvas against the light. Small and seemingly unimportant pinholes in sizing and priming coats cause a certain weakness in the ground because they allow free access of the oil into the weave.

Gelatine glue size is used in the same manner as the rabbitskin glue size. Gelatine glue is simply the ordinary household gelatine used for making desserts.

Use 4 tablespoonfuls of the gelatine to 1 pint of hot water. Stir until dissolved. (The contents of 4 envelopes, or 4 tablespoonfuls equals 1 ounce—the accepted standard for making the size.) Like other glues, gelatine is quickly spoiled by boiling. Once dissolved it is ready.

Masonite panels need a light sandpapering before sizing to roughen the hard, pressed surface, for better adhesion. The application of the size is the same as for canvas. To prevent warping, panels are sized twice on *each* side. The first coat is allowed to dry out before the second coat is brushed on, with a light sandpapering between coats.

Priming. The thoroughly dried sized canvas or Masonite panel is primed with two coats of white lead. I find Dutch Boy White Lead very good for this purpose as it is ground in pure raw linseed oil.

White lead ground in raw linseed oil comes in cans holding from 1 to 100 pounds.

Remove enough white lead from the can to make two coats for your painting surface. Place the pigment on a piece of plate glass or heavy window glass, and break up any lumps with a putty knife or spatula.

One part of damar varnish mixed with 9 parts of turpentine, or turpentine alone, is used for thinning the white lead to priming consistency. Add the thinner in small amounts at a time until the mixture is creamy smooth. To test the consistency, pick some up on a spatula and shake it off gently; some mixture should still hang on. In fresco plastering the same kind of test is made with the trowel to determine the condition of the mortar.

At this stage the white lead is ready to be spread over the sized canvas. With a brush, or household sponge with square-cut edges, the primer is spread evenly over the surface, stopping an inch from the edges. Either the spatula or triangle is used for scraping off the surplus, wiping off the tool on the edges of the canvas. To keep the inner edge of the stretcher from making imprints in the primer, slip a piece of cardboard under the canvas. Scrutinize the surface for ridges left by the scraper and for pinholes in the texture. Dab a little of the primer over the pinholes and scrape again.

The first priming coat should dry for approximately twenty-four hours before the second coating is put on. Both coats are applied in the same fashion. If a regular white-lead-mixed underpainting is contemplated, a second priming coat is not necessary, provided the first one is even and correctly done.

Colored Painting Grounds. Sometimes, to serve a certain purpose, the ground is given a color tone mixed directly with the priming white.

For landscapes, a contrasting rose-gray is produced by mixing Alizarin Crimson, Cobalt Blue or Ultramarine Blue and Yellow Ochre with the primer. A contrasting green-gray for figure painting is made from Cobalt or Ultramarine Blue and Yellow Ochre.

The tube colors are first thinned a little with turpentine in a can, and stirred before they are poured into the primer, making sure that they are thoroughly mixed.

Generally, several canvases or panels are prepared at the same time. In warm weather the glue size will not keep very long and should, for practical reasons, be used up. Sized material should also be promptly primed to protect the size coat.

The mechanism of ground preparation runs as follows: The sizing protects the canvas from the oil in the primer. Again, the primer gives the sizing full protection against the moisture in the air. Together, they build up a very durable foundation for the colors and establish perfect balance in the painting ground.

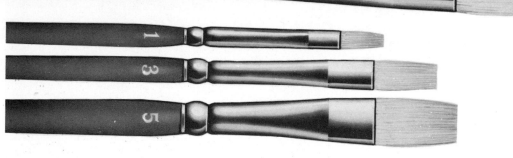

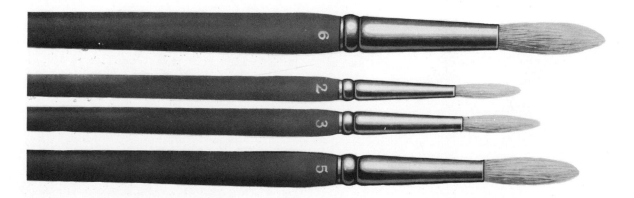

Three groups of bristle brushes: Brights, top; Flats, center; Rounds, bottom. All are actual size.

Chapter 2

Brushes

Bristle and Sable Hair are two main types of brushes used in oil painting. Bristle brushes are made from hog hair and have a nice stiff springiness particularly well suited to brushing out the heavier oil colors. Sable brushes are springy, too, but much softer and more flexible. The textures produced correspond to the characteristics of the brushes used.

Bristle brushes are made in three standard shapes: brights, flat and thin with short bristles; flats, similar to brights but with long bristles; and rounds, with long bristles set in a round ferrule and coming to a point at the tip. Sable hair brushes are also made in brights and rounds.

A fourth shape, the filbert, or portrait oval, is a flat, thicker oval brush of either sable or bristle. For portrait painting, brushes with soft bristles are generally selected.

Brushes vary in width from one-eighth of an inch to 2 inches; sizes are indicated by numbers, ranging from #00 to #20.

Lettering brushes are made of either sable or ox hair. They are soft and springy, and slightly longer than other kinds. The hair is set into a round ferrule, and has a square cut tip.

The size I recommend for drawing in oil, contouring, and so forth, is #6 for average-size paintings, and #9 for large ones.

Inexpensive ox hair brushes are made in most standard shapes and sizes. Among them, the beginner will find many suitable substitutes for the expensive sable hair brushes.

The blender is a round brush made of fluffy badger hair. Primarily the tool of the old school of realistic painting, it is used to fuse one tone with the next, softening the brushwork. The example shown here was painted to illustrate this point. The only texture which shows is that of the canvas surface, and this would not be visible if the paint had been laid on thickly.

Portrait Ovals, or Filberts. At the top are two No. 6 brushes, one long and one short.

The Dutch painter, Vermeer (1632–1675), used a blender to soft-focus the light and objects in the foreground of his paintings. The effect he created is similar to a photograph made with a wide lens opening; the objects in the foreground are soft and fuzzy, and as the distance increases, everything becomes sharper until the depth of sharp focus is reached. Our eyes do the same thing. If we focus them at a distant point, the foreground details are not sharp.

By skillful blending, Vermeer made the foreground objects fuzzy and out of focus, giving the observer the impression of looking *into* instead of just looking *at* his pictures.

Another master of the blender is the contemporary painter, Salvador Dali. Wielding this bushy haired tool over his canvas with great skill, he can accomplish infinitely fine blending.

The blender was used in the painting above to produce the soft focus effect in the foreground objects. A large, badger hair blender is shown at the right at actual size.

However, soft focusing and blending may be overdone and become a mere display of skill and mannerism.

The technique of using the blender is very simple. The brush is held upright, barely touching the color film, and twirled with one or both hands.

Blending and fusing the tones in the manner of the old masters can be achieved with little effort if the #3 medium has been mixed with the colors.

Since the blender is a very sensitive tool, it must be carefully washed with soap after use if it is to be kept in working condition. The brush can be twirled rapidly after rinsing to speed up drying. Hang or stand it free of other tools to keep its fluffy shape.

Blenders come in several sizes. Buy a small one, and find out first if it is the tool for you before you invest in an expensive collection.

When purchasing your initial assortment of brushes, it is wise to buy two or more of each size suggested. When you are painting, you will find that you need a certain size and shape brush for two opposing colors. If you have at least two brushes of the same kind, you will avoid the trouble and delay of constantly washing the same brush between dips back and forth into the two colors.

To start, the student needs only a few bristle flats and brights, selected from sizes #3 to #12; two or three bristle rounds, sizes #4, #9, and #12; two round sable brushes, sizes #9 and #10; three or four flat ox hair brushes, ⅛, ¼, ½, and ¾ inch wide; and one lettering brush about ⅛ inch wide.

On the subject of cost, it is wiser to buy a good quality brush, if not the very best. There is a great difference between "student quality" and professional quality.

A poor tool, while it is no excuse for poor work, does retard the user. A student of oil painting has so much to learn that he should not place unnecessary obstacles in his path by using inferior tools and materials.

From the very first, try to use the larger, broader brushes for a speedy summing up of the color impressions. This will keep the all-over painting tonality from falling apart due to indecisive painting. Using only the smaller brushes throughout a painting may give it an irresolute and ragged look. Small brushes are for setting in detail, for covering small areas, and so forth.

The round bristle brushes are useful for long, unbroken strokes. The rounds hold more color and facilitate a longer stroke.

Dexterous painting is done from the wrist to the tip of the brush. Use the whole length of

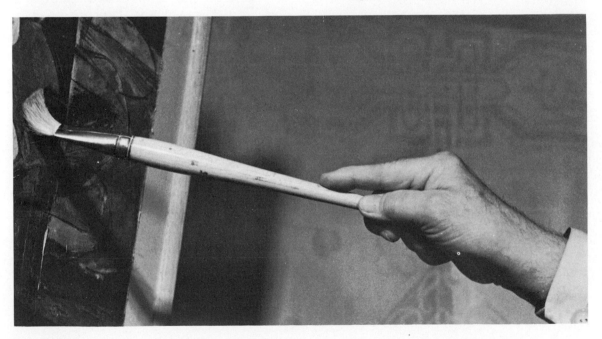

the arm, or the arm from the elbow, to change the position of the brush over the canvas.

For complete freedom of movement, learn to hold the brush with all the fingers closed about the end of the handle. Steer the brush with the index finger stretched out on the handle, the end resting against the inside of the hand, in much the same way that an engraver holds a burin. Heavier brushes can be held firmly in this way for painting over a large surface. The other type of finger grip should also be at the end of the handle (see illustrations).

The pointed round sable brushes, and the lettering brush are the tools necessary for outlining, drawing, and setting in small, sharp details of a picture.

The 10-inch length of the handle, common to oil painting brushes, must not be cut. Shortening the handle just about ends its usefulness as a good painting tool.

For reasons that I have not been able to fathom, brush handles have been made shorter in recent years, to the great detriment of their balance.

If a special shape brush is needed to suit a particular purpose, find one in your art store. Don't try to reshape one. Trying to give a brush a haircut takes more skill than the average person possesses, and should not be attempted.

Cleaning and care of the brushes. To keep brushes in shape and in good working condition, they must be scrupulously cleaned after use. Before washing in soap and water, rinse them out in turpentine or kerosene to reduce the paint, and then wipe with newspaper or a rag.

Flax soap, the well-known soft oil soap, or the equally good yellow naptha soap are both suitable for brush washing. After rinsing with turpentine, take several brushes in one hand and with the other hand squeeze soap into the roots of the brushes. If color is allowed to collect and dry at the bottom of the bristles, it will soon build up a hard crust of paint and spoil the brush. Should this happen, or if a brush full of paint is left to dry and becomes hard, use one of the several good brush cleaners on the market. After the softening up, the brush must be

Oxhair lettering brush, actual size

washed with soap to bring back the springiness of the bristle.

Only lukewarm or cold water should be used for washing. Hot water may spoil a brush by causing the bristle to curl and fluff up.

Do not stand a brush upright on the bristles in a can of turpentine or kerosene, as the bristles will bend out of shape. This is a barbaric practice, deplored by every craftsman with pride in his tools. If you find it necessary for any reason to stand a brush in a can, bristles down, tilt the can so that the pressure on the bristles is relieved.

There are several brush rinsers on the market, designed for rapid rinsing of brushes. The artist can make a cheap and very effective one (*see illustration*).

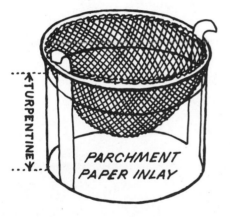

Home-made brush rinser

Buy a wire mesh tea strainer, and a jar with an opening large enough to hold the strainer snugly. Cut a piece of parchment paper into a circle the size of the bottom of the jar, leaving two strips to project upward and over the sides as shown.

Fit the paper circle snugly over the bottom of the jar, with the paper strips extending upward so that they can be held in place by the wire strainer. Place the strainer over the mouth of the jar. Pour turpentine into the jar so that only a part of the wire mesh dips into the liquid.

To use, dip the brush in the turpentine to the bottom of the strainer and then gently run the brush up the sides of the mesh to wash out the paint. Repeat the process until the brush is clean; then wipe with a rag and you will have a clean brush ready for use.

After the rinser has been in use for some time, let it stand until the paint settles to the bottom and the turpentine is clarified. Remove the strainer, carefully pour off the clarified turpentine into another jar, lift up the parchment circle by the side strips and scrape it clean with a palette knife. Wipe the jar with a rag, and wipe off any residue left on the paper. Then wipe the strainer and replace all the parts. Pour the clarified turpentine back, adding more so that the level is the same as before, and your rinser is back in business.

You may want to make two rinsers, one for your small brushes, and a larger one for your large brushes. I find the two sizes very convenient.

To sum up, the best way to take care of your brushes is simply to rinse them out in turpentine, then wash them in soap and water and rinse them in clear water as soon as painting is over for the day. Squeeze out the rinsing water with a rag and shape, or "dress," the bristle. Tin cans weighted down with gravel make fine brush holders.

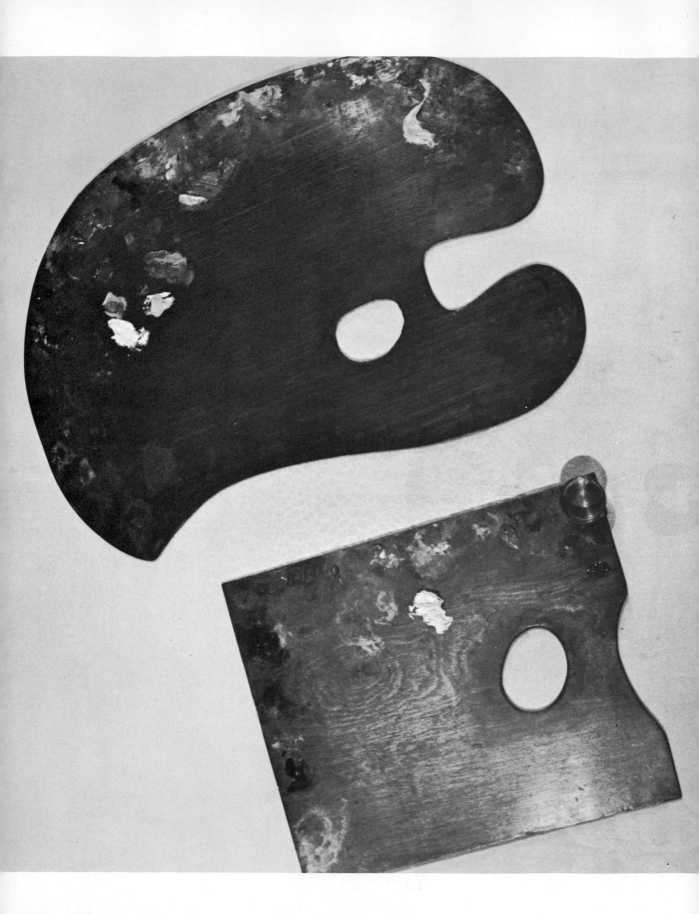

Chapter 3

Miscellaneous Equipment

Palettes. Rectangular palettes are fitted into most paint boxes. For studio work, the large-size oval, or similarly shaped palettes, are favored. Painting tables on casters, with stationary palette, drawers for colors, brushes, and painting implements, are widely used. The kind of palette or painting arrangement you use is a matter of personal taste and feeling.

I have owned a painting table for twenty years. It has a very practical large palette and every convenience, and still I never use it as a palette or for setting up colors. I find it too stationary, better suited for holding painting utensils than for a rolling table palette. The French idea of a systematic use of several palettes is a better solution for me. In my work I use four or five palettes. I set up a large studio palette with my own range and arrangement of colors. The others are more or less separate mixing boards, one for cool shades, another for warm, the next for dark and deep tonalities, and so forth. Since the deepest tones are the ones most likely to be spoiled by accidental contact with the lighter ones, the convenience of having separate palettes is obvious. Wrong mixtures can easily be removed or mixed over again, without running into other colors nearby. By the systematic use of separate palettes there is less danger of having the colors break down to a grayish half-tone which invariably happens on a crowded palette.

Palettes should be as light and strong as possible. My two oldest palettes are 51 and 49 years old, and are still constantly in use. They are made of walnut wood less than ⅛-inch thick, well balanced, with a large opening for the thumb. My other two rectangular palettes are also made of walnut. The large studio palette is made of a 3-ply macassar ebony, also less than ⅛-inch thick. The dark color of the palettes does not bother me since I always try out the shades, one against the other, on a sheet of white paper.

Whether one or five palettes are used for painting a picture, it is important to keep them in top condition. Always clean off the mixings that are not going to be used further. An extra palette, whether working at home or in a studio, greatly increases the efficiency and the quality of the work.

Palette Cup. Used for holding the painting medium, it is clamped to one corner of the palette. The cup should be wide enough for medium-size brushes. The easily cleaned straight-sided cup is preferred. Cups with inverted sides are hard to keep clean. For the larger brushes a large can standing within reach is more practical. If a cup is too small for a brush, it will ruin the bristles by bending them out of shape.

Put only a small amount of medium in the cup. Replenish with fresh medium several times during the painting period. Before filling the cup with fresh medium, the residue on the bottom must be wiped out. Medium that still remains in

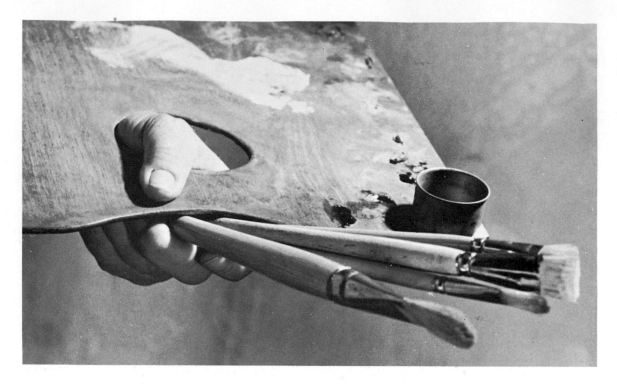

This photograph shows correct finger grip on palette and brushes.

the cup after the work is ended must be thrown away and not used again. Any medium left standing with free access to the air will become unfit for color thinning in a few hours, particularly after it has been stirred with the brushes. I repeat what I said earlier in this series—the oxidizing effect of the air is supposed to take place in the color film of the painting, not in the medium cup.

Palette Knife. Inseparable from the palette this knife is useful for mixing colors, cleaning the palette, and scraping down areas in the painting to a thin layer, as well as for applying paint. A straight knife and a trowel-shaped knife are the most practical. The trowel shape is especially well adapted for knife painting. For the beginner these two are adequate for any kind of work.

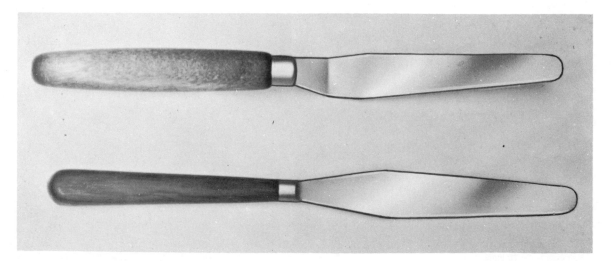

Here are a few of the many shapes of painting knives.

Palettes and knives encrusted with old hard paint can be cleaned and restored with paint remover. Before using paint remover read the information on the label carefully. All loosened paint is scraped off the palette with the palette knife, and the surface washed clean with turpentine and dried. When completely dry, the wood is given a polish with newspaper, or a rag, and raw linseed oil. Both sides are treated in this way to keep the wood from warping. Remember that paint rags and waste soaked with drying oils, colors or removers are inflammable and must be handled sensibly.

Paint Box. A new kind of paint box of wood or aluminum, with or without an easel, seems to appear on the market almost every year.

Select one according to personal taste and economy. A light roomy box, and a rigid, strong easel of the field type, is all that is needed for a good start. Some of the box-easel combinations are good for studio work. The large and expensive French-type studio easel, geared for moving the canvas higher or lower, is, of course, the "dream easel," but no good as a starter in buy-

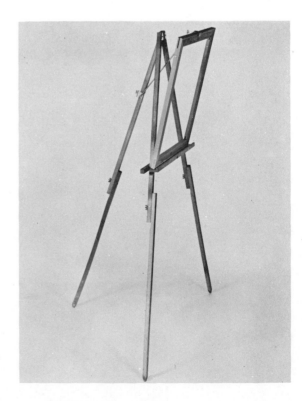

A portable, folding easel

ing painting equipment. Money saved on less expensive implements should be used for buying the more essential colors, brushes and canvas.

Hand Rest (maulstick). For small detail and close-up work a hand rest is needed. A 3- foot length of bamboo, or one made from light weight wood and tapered, is the best. The small end is provided with a wooden knob and should be covered with a couple of layers of clean rags tied with a piece of cord. Each time the rag becomes too soiled, it should be replaced.

Chapter 4

Tube Colors

Oil colors in tubes are generally ground by roller mills, or similar machinery; a few are still ground by hand. Some of the colors are manufactured from earth pigments, others from artificial iron oxides. An assortment of shades, called tints, are dyes precipitated on fillers to give them body so they can be ground into paste and squeezed into tubes.

The artificial iron oxides have replaced many of the earth colors. They do not have the natural transparency found in the earth colors, but are more opaque. Natural siennas and ochres are still available to the artist. Raw sienna is a transparent pigment of a golden hue. Strong heat treatment turns it into a deep reddish brown: *Burnt Sienna*. This color is well known for its many fine qualities, great strength, and deep transparency, important to tonalities of unusual depth. Because of its ability to penetrate, or "bleed through," Burnt Sienna should not be used in thick fat underlayers. This bleeding through will not occur in mixtures with other colors.

One of the earliest pigments known is *Yellow Ochre*. This natural pigment cannot be imitated successfully by an iron oxide, and gives a special quality of tone and feeling to mixtures with other colors. For example, mixing genuine Yellow Ochre with Ivory Black and white will produce a warm gray, while an artificial ochre makes the mixture look greenish. For rendering the colors in a landscape, or the airiness of the sky, Yellow Ochre has no equal. The elusive flesh tones of the human body are found in graduations of Yellow Ochre from cool to warm.

Cadmium Yellow, light, and *Cadmium Yellow, deep,* are outstanding when rich clear yellows and greens are needed for effective contrasts in a painting. Genuine Cadmium Yellow is more expensive than its artificial imitations or substitutes. However, the imitations cannot compare with the genuine pigment for effectiveness, and do not have its high saturation. This alone makes up for the cost of the better product.

Cadmium Red, light, because of its brilliancy has found wide use in depicting the intensity of light, for example, where direct sunlight saturates prominent areas and creates strong contrasts of light and shade. In figure painting, a similar, effective, intense feeling of strong light may be achieved by Cadmium Red, light, when used in contrast with the surrounding color areas.

Rose Madder, painted in a very light, translucent tone, will also act as a reflector of light. It can be employed equally well in the deep values of darkness.

The color brilliancy of *Alizarin Madder* lends itself to light and airy shades of violet and purple, especially as cool contrasts to other warmer colors in the foreground.

Grumbacher *Alizarin Crimson, Golden,* is a new shade of Crimson, between the cool shade of ordinary Crimson and Rose Madder. In Rose mixtures, this brand imparts very useful, soft, warm tints of red.

Genuine *Cobalt Blue* is one of the most durable of the blue colors, stable in all techniques. A good drier, Cobalt Blue is of particular value in underpainting. The color belongs in the light tints of the azure. It has little opacity, and readily lends itself to transparent atmospheric effects.

Ultramarine Blue is a very stable artificial product with high saturation. In contrast to Cobalt Blue, its place is in the heavier parts of the painting, where it has a strong influence on the light.

The *Phthalocyanine Blue,* or for short *Cyan Blue,* has a tremendously high saturation and needs toning down with white, loosely mixed. However, only a small amount of white should be used to avoid throwing the mixture out of kilter. Another caution: due to its high saturation, even a tiny overdose of the blue will spoil the color tone, forcing one to remix. This clear neutral blue is enormously useful in mixing all kinds of greens. For example, emerald green, the green color seen in the spectrum, can be closely imitated by mixing Cyan Blue, Viridian and Cadmium Yellow, light. *Permanent Emerald Green* approximates the color of such a mixture.

Deep, unadulterated *Viridian* is one of the few greens wholly dependable in all techniques. Cool, as well as warm tonalities, in shadow or in light, are quickly achieved by using Viridian as the basic green. Unaffected by other colors, it will hold its tone indefinitely in the lightest tints as well as the deepest darks.

The Three Whites: White Lead, Zinc White, and Titanium White. Still in universal use by artists is the white of ancient times—*White Lead,* a basic carbonate of lead. It was known and used by artists long before oil painting had made any contribution to art. Thanks to its remarkable properties, it has probably saved whole periods of painting from extinction. *Flake White* and *Cremnitz White* are names for white lead put up in tubes.

White lead is poisonous in powder form, and dangerous to inhale. Ground in oil in tubes, it can be handled with full safety. However, like most modern house paints, it should not be allowed to stay on the skin for any length of time. Cleanliness is in order when handling any kind of paint.

This tough, strong color is a fast drier, opaque with good covering properties. As a primer over canvas size it makes the surface impervious to most causes of color deterioration. As the basic white in all underpainting, it has no equal. It is also valuable in building up textures throughout a painting. Only such a stable, strong pigment can be counted upon to hold and keep a textured surface intact.

Only whites ground in raw linseed oil should be used in underpainting and in the underlayers of the color film.

Flake White and Cremnitz White are good driers in themselves and are typical underpainting whites. Because of their natural fast-drying properties, they produce a hard, firm base in the underlayers.

But if they are ground in slow-drying oils, such as poppy oil, the drying and hardening could be slowed down for weeks before it would be safe to paint over them. Even in "wet in wet," alla prima painting, a slow-drying white is not particularly helpful since the painting is done in one sitting. All such slow-drying colors should be left to the experts.

Grumbacher Pre-tested Flake White #562, ground in raw linseed oil, has all the good properties necessary for successful underpainting and color mixtures in the underlayers. Because of its fast hardening property, this paint is sold only in studio-size tubes.

Zinc White. This oxide of zinc is nonpoisonous. Transparent only to a degree, it serves as a mixing white, and is safe with all colors. It takes a little longer to dry than white lead and therefore should be used in the upper layers. Well made, and ground with oils of normal drying and hardening qualities, Zinc White is perhaps the easiest white to handle.

Titanium White. This titanium dioxide white is whiter than the two others. Although it has been in existence only a little over thirty years, this white has found favor among artists. Because of its high density and pure whiteness, Titanium White is very useful where sharp white opaqueness is wanted for sharp contrasts in value. As a straight white it has none of the outstanding features of the other whites, such as strong adhesiveness or the property of producing a hard tough color surface. It is decidedly not an underpainting white.

Half-White, a color often mentioned in this series, is seldom found as a tube color. It is usually mixed by the painter himself, from equal parts of Zinc White and white lead. The white lead may be either Flake White or Cremnitz White. (*See color spread.*)

Chapter 5

Painting Mediums and Thinners

What shall the painter use to dilute his colors? This has been a vexing question throughout the history of oil painting.

The few formulas handed down to us, and the evidence supplied by some paintings, have helped us gain a great deal of knowledge. The most important fact we have learned is that improper use of either thinner or medium will cause yellowing and darkening. A good rule to remember is—use more discretion and less thinner or medium.

Turpentine has held its place as a good thinner among artists and rightly so, if only the best brands available are used. Rectified Oil of Turpentine, distilled over several times, and Gum Spirit of Turpentine, both high-grade products distilled from the gum of trees, are the only turpentines that can be safely used as thinners and for making up mediums. I have found the T & R brand of Pure Spirits of Gum Turpentine, manufactured by Turpentine and Rosin Factors, Inc., to be of the highest possible quality. The cheaper commercial brands of turpentine are chiefly housepaint thinners, distilled from wood chips, not from the gum. This type of turpentine will form a dark, sticky sediment if left with free access to air. The sediment, if allowed to mix with underlayers, may stay soft or half-dried for a long time; the upper layers, with the help of a fast-drying color pigment, will harden first, and cracking is sure to follow.

Turpentine alone, employed in painting, acts as a strong diluent lowering the adhesive quality of the colors. If you use still stronger diluting agents like Essence of Petroleum, or Benzine and others, in overdoses, the colors will crumble from lack of adhesive strength, and dust off after drying. However, this will not happen if these stronger diluents are used with moderation and the colors are painted out thinly over a lean, hard canvas ground. Runs and puddles should not be left, for they will show up clearly in the drying of the colors, causing shiny markings on the surface.

Mediums containing oil, varnish, and turpentine have been used throughout the history of oil painting. In spite of the fact that the early oils, varnishes, and turpentines, were different from our factory-made kinds, these basic materials are still used in much the same way today.

Raw linseed oil is an indispensable ingredient. It must be of the highest quality, specially prepared for the painter's use. Bleached oil is not necessary, and polymerized oil should never, under any circumstances, be allowed to find its way into a painting. This type is processed for entirely different purposes.

Damar Varnish and *Mastic Varnish* are important ingredients of painting mediums and can be easily prepared by the artist. Damar and mastic are soft resins, readily dissolved in turpentine. They can be purchased at chemical supply houses, drug stores, and the better equipped art stores, although the latter usually carry them ready-mixed for use. The resins come in the form of drops, or tears.

To prepare your own varnish, take 2¾ ounces of damar or mastic resin drops and mix with about 1/3 the volume of bird gravel. Put this mixture in a piece of cheesecloth and tie it to form a small bag. Pour 1 pint of turpentine into a wide-mouthed jar, big enough to hold the bag. Suspend the bag in the turpentine so that it does not touch the bottom of the jar.

Put the jar in a warm place, and leave it undisturbed for about two weeks until the resin is completely dissolved in the turpentine. The bird gravel clears the resin from dust particles and from the insoluble residue sometimes found in gums.

Pour the finished varnish into small bottles of convenient size, and label "Full Strength Damar Varnish," giving the formula used. Discard the bag, gravel, and jar. When the time comes to make another batch of varnish, use new, clean utensils.

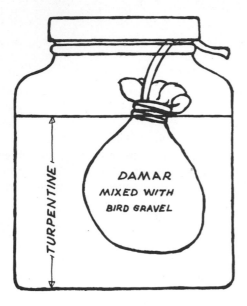

VARNISH MAKING ARRANGEMENT

Both damar and mastic varnishes should be used with dry tools over a dry surface in a dry room. Humidity and moisture will cause "blueing," or a "bloom" on the varnished surface.

Intermediate Varnish, or *Retouching Varnish* is a lean mixture of 1 part damar varnish and 3 parts of turpentine. This varnish is brushed out thinly over the entire surface of a dry underpainting. Also, colors that have sunk, or drawn back, leaving mat spots, can be brought out by brushing a thin coat of the varnish over them, wiping the surplus off with a clean rag.

Carefully following this procedure throughout the painting will keep the colors at full strength, and fresh. The painter should wait until the underlying surface is dry enough to leave a pale white line when scratched with the fingernail—an old house painter's trick to test undercoatings for dryness and hardness.

Sun-thickened Oil was one of the important ingredients in the sixteenth century Flemish painting mediums, used in combinations with varnishes and balsams. It can be bought in art stores, ready to use, or it can be easily made. Three simple implements are needed: a ½-inch-deep white enamel pan, commonly seen in butcher shops; two ½-inch-thick strips of wood, 6 inches longer than the width of the pan; and a piece of window glass large enough to overlap the pan.

The pan is filled with high-grade raw linseed oil. The pieces of wood are placed across the pan to keep the glass ½ inch above the tray, giving free access to the air. Place the pan in the sun. From time to time stir the oil to test the thickness. Sun-thickened oil should be allowed to become almost the same consistency as honey.

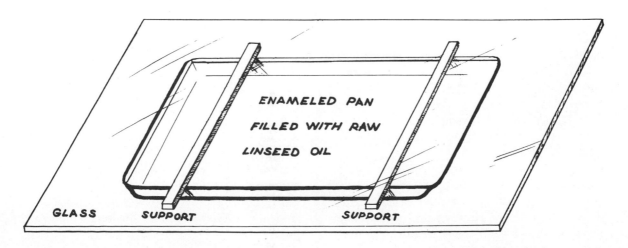

IMPLEMENTS FOR MAKING SUN-THICKENED OIL

A few sunny days will complete the thickening process. Then the oil is strained through a piece of muslin or organdy tied over the top of a clean can to remove insects and small debris. The finished oil is poured into a bottle with a wide neck, closed tight and labeled.

For a heavy medium, use less turpentine with the sun-thickened oil. The colors embedded in such a medium dry with a pleasant sheen, and generally do not need protective varnishing.

MEDIUM FORMULAS.

Three medium formulas are given here and used in the exercises in this series, *"Course in Beginning Oil Painting."* Although there are many other formulas, these three are all I consider necessary for a beginner.

A practical bottle for making up and storing the mediums should have a wide neck and an airtight cover.

A paper strip, as shown in the accompanying illustration, giving the proportions of the ingredients, should be pasted on the bottle. It will identify the medium, and also provide a ready reminder of its formula. Keep the bottle tightly closed and upright between each filling of the palette cup. Remember to shake it before using.

Medium #1: One part of artists' quality raw linseed oil mixed with two parts of turpentine. This is the thinnest of the formulas, and will leave only a slight sheen after the colors are dried. It is used in "wet in wet" painting, as it will not "set up" and start the drying process as fast as the others.

Medium #2: One part of raw linseed oil, 1 part of damar, or mastic varnish, and 1½ parts of turpentine shaken together. The varnish in this mixture will make the paint dry and harden faster than the first formula, leaving a more glossy, agreeable sheen on the dried surface.

Medium #3: One part sun-thickened oil, 1 part damar varnish, and 1½ to 2 parts turpentine, depending on the thickness of the oil. The drying period is slightly longer for this mixture; it dries a little more glossy than #2. The enamel-like surface is agreeable and does not appear unpleasantly greasy. After thorough hardening, it will retain its surface sheen; rubbed with a soft rag it becomes even glossier.

These formulas can be modified by using more turpentine if a thinner consistency is desired. Remember that mediums are generally adjusted to suit a particular technique. However, to avoid the possibility of darkening, do not use more than one part of linseed oil.

Driers are not necessary in easel pictures. Instead, Flake or Cremnitz White is mixed half-and-half with Zinc White and employed as a painting white in mixtures with rapidly drying colors. Such mixtures dry firm and hard.

Yellow Ochre, Cobalt Blue, Viridian and Alizarin Madder are good driers. Serviceable underpainting can be done with them with little effort. They should be loosely painted, mixed with white in light and airy shades.

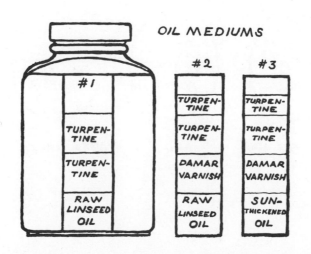

OIL MEDIUMS

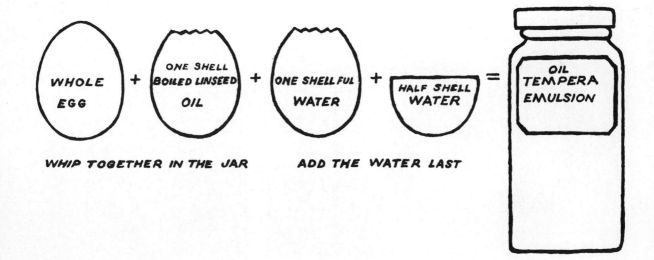

WHOLE EGG + ONE SHELL BOILED LINSEED OIL + ONE SHELLFUL WATER + HALF SHELL WATER = OIL TEMPERA EMULSION

WHIP TOGETHER IN THE JAR   ADD THE WATER LAST

Chapter 6

Tempera

Long before medieval times, egg tempera was used as the binder for pigments in painting on wood panels. Sometimes even fresco murals were touched up or partly repainted in tempera colors.

The discovery of emulsifying the egg with oil or varnish was important in hastening the arrival of true oil painting. When egg yolk alone or the whole egg was diluted with water only, it became hard to handle; if this binder was too rich, it cracked; if too lean, it dusted off.

The egg-oil emulsion is less sensitive and a very practical binder-vehicle. Well dried, it is impervious to most of the causes of deterioration of the color film; it combines readily with the oil colors, either on a half-dried, tacky, or a dry surface, especially when the #2 and #3 painting mediums have been used to dilute the colors.

The fifteenth century Italian and Dutch painters made extensive use of tempera white for practical and effective underpainting, erasure, repainting, and so forth. What in some cases looks like heavy impasto of oil colors is actually a skillfully applied tempera underpainting, overpainted in resinous oil color painted out in transparent or semi-opaque coats. Damar or mastic varnish medium was the regularly accepted thinner.

In some of the Dutch masters' work it is exceedingly hard to tell where the tempera white begins and ends. In places where the tempera white was set directly into the wet or sticky oil color film and painted over again, the fusion between the two media was complete and is invisible.

The beginning of the eighteenth century saw a decline in the use of tempera and the careful building up of the color surface. However, unwise use of unstable color pigments, in particular the notoriously bad Asphalt Brown, ruined not only many of the paintings but much of the entire technique of oil painting. Series of unstable pigments cluttered up the color catalogues and handbooks. All sorts of media were recommended. Colors and mediums too rich in oil probably contributed greatly in hastening the ruin of many otherwise fine paintings. When Asphalt Brown was mixed into the color film it cracked in wide fissures and slowly slipped downward over the painting. Rembrandt sometimes used Asphalt Brown, but only as a last very thin glazing and thus avoided such mishaps. Knowing the dangerous behavior of Asphalt Brown, he usually applied a brown color known as Mummy Brown, supposedly made from ground-up mummies. Today, Asphalt Brown is obsolete as an artist's color and is rarely used.

In the early nineteenth century Hans von Marées (1837–1887) attempted to bring back sound methods of oil painting by going back to tempera painting and resinous oil colors. With an egg emulsion, slightly different than that in use today, he revived one of the most stable methods of oil painting, the so-called "mixed method" of tempera underpainting combined with resinous oil color overpainting. His paintings and his style are remarkably close to our time in feeling and expression.

OIL TEMPERA EMULSION FORMULAS.

Formula #1: Make an opening at the top of a fresh egg (*see illustration*), puncture the yolk and empty the whole egg into a glass jar previously rinsed with boiling water. Beat the egg with a long bristle brush. An egg beater should not be used; it is too harsh for making a usable emulsion.

Fill the empty shell with real *boiled linseed oil,* empty into the jar and beat the egg and the oil together thoroughly, again using a long bristle brush. Pour 1½ shellfuls of tap water, or distilled water, into the jar. Close the jar tightly with the cover and shake all the ingredients together.

In order to keep the emulsion fresh as long as possible, add 4 or 5 drops of turpentine or oil of cloves and mix thoroughly. Label the jar with the formula used. Keep the jar closed tight.

To make a perfect emulsion, the boiled linseed oil must be a true boiled oil, not oil of the type nicknamed "bung hole boiled," which is heated and fixed with a drier. Such doctored oils are useless for making an emulsion.

The true boiled linseed oil is a golden brown color and has a pungent pleasant odor all its own. If it is too hard to find, the following formula can be used:

Formula #2: Proceed as before, using the eggshell as a measuring receptacle and, instead of the boiled oil, mix equal parts of raw linseed oil and full strength damar varnish together. Empty one shell measure of this mixture into the beaten egg and beat the two together to form an emulsion. One and a half shells of water are added and the mixture is shaken together as previously described. The mixing sequence cannot be altered and still make a successful emulsion. Also, the emulsion must be shaken thoroughly, every time, before it is used in mixing the tempera white.

TEMPERA WHITE.

Powdered Zinc White and Titanium White are the white pigments generally used for making tempera white. They combine easily with the emulsion to form a homogeneous white color.

For the color receptacle, select a 4-ounce jar with a wide opening and a twist-off cover. Before use, rinse out the jar and the cover in boiling water.

To make the white, pour in two tablespoons of the shaken emulsion and stir in enough of the powdered Zinc White to form a smooth color, not quite as heavy as tube color in consistency. Stir with a straight palette knife, or one made of wood. A small amount of tempera white should be made up each time, just enough for a few days' work.

Any color collecting on the inside of the cover must be scraped off now and then to keep it from falling into the jar and making the color gritty.

Leftover color in the jar can be kept fresh longer by pouring water into the jar to stand over the white, acting as an extra cover. Pour along the side of the jar to keep the water from mixing and thinning the color. Keep both the color and emulsion jars in a moderately cold place, but not in an icebox as freezing spoils tempera immediately.

Every time you work with tempera, use plenty of tempered water for thinning. To soften or "temper" the water, stir a brush-dip of the white and a teaspoonful of the emulsion into a quart of tap water. The slight cloudiness of the tempered water is beneficial and helpful.

Erasure with tempera white is the quickest and safest way to correct large areas in a fresh painting. The areas to be corrected may be too dark, poorly balanced, or the wrong color. Painting over them could further unbalance the picture. The new colors might mix with the wrong ones, or the underpainting effect might be lost.

To make corrections with tempera white, follow this simple procedure: the fresh oil colors are first scraped off the area to be corrected if they are heavy or dark. Then tempera white is applied and allowed to dry thoroughly. Where the color is light and not too thick, the tempera white is painted directly into the wet oil color. Here, too, it is allowed to dry thoroughly in a warm place. Usually after an hour of drying painting may be resumed over the erasure.

Chapter 7

Glazing

A glaze is a thin, transparent layer of color usually applied over a dry color or underpainting. The painting of a wooden bowl with fruit is shown here to illustrate the effect of glazing on the total color in a picture. Only the left part of the painting has been glazed.

The difference between the glazed and unglazed parts lies not so much in the hues as in the unification of the colors seen as a whole—which is exactly what glazing is meant to do.

This is a realistic painting. The colors are true local colors with warm, reflected light from the orange-brown bowl, gray-blue shadow on the white tablecloth on the dark brown table, and cold blueish light on top of the apples to the right.

The glazing color is mixed from Burnt Sienna and Crimson, with the usual addition of Cremnitz or Flake White, and some Yellow Ochre added to balance the warmth of the shade. Medium #2 works easily in such thinly laid glazes and wiping with a rag leaves few marks if done evenly with no after wiping of lights.

The simple method of applying only one coat of allover glazing is better suited to our present-day style of painting than the old-time method of multiple glazing.

The medium used in the imprimatura is also the medium used for mixing the glazing color.

Any of the colors on our palette can be used. Especially good glazing colors are: Viridian, Ultramarine Blue, Cobalt Blue, Cyan Blue, Yellow Ochre, Cadmium Yellow, deep, Rose Madder, Alizarin Crimson, Burnt Sienna and Ivory Black. Before making a glaze with Rose Madder and Alizarin Crimson, they are mixed with a little Flake or Cremnitz White to give them more body stability. Since glaze is quick setting, and fast drying, it should be applied reasonably fast with a moderately stiff brush. Sometimes when an uneven toning is desired, a rag will give good service. For a perfectly even tone, the finger tips or the ball of the hand may be used to apply the color.

Regarding the color tone, it is advisable to use glazes that will not make the underlying colors of similar hues look overly hot or icy cold. Exaggeration in either direction may hurt the painting beyond repair. A slight adjustment of the tonality is the real purpose, not a repainting job.

One of the most frequent mishaps in this type of work is glazing over a spotty or poorly dried surface. Such a disaster can really be disheartening.

Chapter 8

Short or Long Oil Color

The terms *short* or *lean* and *long* or *fat* are used to describe the viscosity of the oil colors.

The addition of oil, damar, or mastic varnish makes the color long, or fat. By adding sun-thickened oil, as in medium #3, the color is made still more viscous, or longer.

Oil colors thinned with turpentine or medium #1 are short or lean. The heavy, opaque, Flake and Cremnitz Whites are in themselves short colors. Titanium White is also to some extent considered short.

Short, lean colors dry with little gloss. They are ground in raw linseed oil which has been previously shortened by the addition of water, drop by drop, and shaken. In my apprentice days this was done by hand, and I have seen it done in Paris, in places where artists' tube colors are still hand ground. The shortened oil is used mostly for interior ornamental painting.

The long or fat mediums make the color surface dry to a more or less glossy finish, depending on the proportion of oil and varnish in the mixture. In this category are the typical glazing colors, the colors used in overpainting tempera, and the optic grays. In general, they are the colors producing transparent depth in painting, as seen in the works of the old masters.

Thinning with turpentine makes the color not only short, but also less adhesive. I have pointed out throughout this series that the thinning mediums must be used with restraint and intelligent understanding of their characteristics. Because of the decreased adhesiveness peculiar to turpentine, this thinner must be used with the greatest restraint. If a mat surface is desired, use mat colors specially prepared for this purpose so that adherence to the priming will be insured.

Chapter 9

Painting "Alla Prima"

I have mentioned this technique at various times in this series and have given several examples and exercises. The term, *alla prima,* simply means to complete a painting "at once" or at one sitting. It is the technique of painting wet in wet—painting into the wet underlayers until the picture is finished. When much of the technical knowledge of the old masters disappeared, in the early 1800's, painters were forced to paint alla prima in order to eliminate the dangers of working over partly dried places in their pictures. The technique was looked upon as a real feat.

This technique produces pictures full of freshness and spontaneity. It teaches a discipline of great importance—you must know at all times just what you are going to do with the painting tools. It will show up aimless or irresolute painting faster than any other method.

To familiarize himself with painting alla prima the beginner should not start with anything more ambitious than a simple still life. The technique requires much faster action and greater determination than the normally slower painting over dry underlayers.

A hard, non-absorbent canvas and fairly thick colors are used in alla prima painting.

Form and shadow are rapidly indicated by drawing with the brush in dark, neutral, warm black in broad lines. The shadows are left slightly narrower than their final size, and more transparent than the rest of the drawing.

Each successive development of the picture, however sketchy, should have the appearance of something complete in itself.

Local colors are painted flat and not too close in value and tone to the final color. The painting continues, developing more and more toward its final appearance, leaving the deepest depths and the highlights until the very last.

The type of medium used determines to what extent the painter can continue wet in wet before the surface becomes tacky, or half dry. This is not necessarily disastrous, as the painting can be left to dry and then developed further in another technique.

When the surface becomes tacky, it is not advisable to continue painting alla prima. Persisting will end up in losing the freshness of tone, and will increase the ever-present possibility of darkening and cracking.

For successful painting in this valuable technique, you need a modest-sized canvas, a relatively simple subject, medium #1, and most important, a thorough preparation for the fast, sure-handed work ahead.

Chapter 10

Varnishing the Picture

Paintings in oil colors must be protected with a coat of varnish. Without the protection of either a resinous painting medium, or a top varnish, Cremnitz White will turn gray, and Cadmium Yellows turn white because of their sensitivity to air pollution.

Preliminary or in-between varnish is applied over the painting after the colors have become hard to the touch.

Regular *picture varnish* is laid on as a final protective covering after a drying period of 5 or 6 months, and at least a year for paintings with heavy impasto, to avoid rubbing up layers of color which have not entirely hardened.

Preliminary varnish made from the light, transparent damar or mastic varnish is excellent, thinned in the proportion of 1 part varnish to 3 or 4 parts of turpentine.

Preliminary varnish can also be used as a temporary final varnish when applied over completely dry paintings. It often lasts for years; and it has this advantage—after the varnish surface has accumulated dirt, the soiled varnish can be removed by friction. The finger tips are rubbed over the surface until the resin is pulverized and can be wiped off dry. The principle is the same as starching newly painted interior walls to protect the paint. When the surface gets dirty, instead of repainting, the starch is washed off, the clean surface underneath laid bare and starched again. The lean, soft resin varnish works much in the same way; it is easily removed without the help of dangerous dissolving agents which may injure the color film.

The varnishing utensils are simple: a good brush with soft bristles about 2 inches wide securely set in the brush, a small saucer, and the varnish bottle.

The picture, varnish bottle, brush, and saucer should be kept together in a warm, dry place for a few hours, to equalize their temperature in order to avoid so-called "bloom"—a blueish, milky deterioration of the varnish surface caused by moisture on the color film. Hot and humid summer days are not the time for varnishing. Dark paintings suffer most from bloom which is hard to eliminate, once produced.

The author at the age of fourteen was apprenticed to a carriage painter and remembers very well the precautions taken to offset costly mishaps in varnishing, common even to the heavy body varnishes made from hard copal resins. An approaching thunderstorm, with sudden change of atmospheric conditions, was enough to stop any attempt to varnish that day.

Before varnishing, dust is removed by slapping the picture with a soft rag. If some of the dust still clings to the surface, it can be rolled off with the soft dough of fresh bread—continuing with fresh dough until all the dust is lifted off. The color surface is wiped lightly with a soft, clean rag to remove any moisture that may still remain.

Varnishing is done in the same manner as the application of size over canvas—with a light hand. Always brush into the nearby wet edge, and avoid slipping over on a setting drying lane. Slowly fill the texture without leaving any pinholes.

If mat spots occur after the varnish has dried, they can be remedied by careful revarnishing of each one to even out the entire surface.

After the final varnish coat has become hard and dustproof, the picture is finished.

A word of caution—picture varnishes must never be used in any of the mediums. They would constitute a real danger, causing the color film to crack.

Chapter 11

Painting Exercises

Training yourself with the help of the exercises in this series calls for ingredients only you can supply—patience and perseverance. Read each exercise, try painting it or a similar scene, and if necessary, do it over until you are satisfied with the result.

After a magnificent performance by a great violinist, one of his admirers said to him, "I would give my life to play like that." The violinist replied, "I did." Remember, as in almost everything, you get out of painting only what you put into it.

The painting methods and techniques described in the exercises are all based on the color range of one palette, although the full range is not always used for any one exercise. While you are studying and painting the exercises, do not attempt to substitute other colors for those given. This will defeat my systematic teaching of the meaning of color.

Try out the chromatic possibilities of the palette as given; this is the best possible way to use this series of books for self-education in oil painting.

Sketch frequently; repeat a sketch often, adding variations, simplifying, and abstracting. Try to extract all the possibilities in the subject matter.

As you gain in proficiency, personal characteristics will emerge with increasing strength and clarity in each successive painting. Be honestly yourself. No one can be any more, and no one should be any less. You will be amazed to see how your paintings will begin to reflect you.

HILLS AND TREES

In this landscape, seen in the diffused light of an overcast sky, harmony is created by using the same shadow color throughout the painting.

The shadow color is a warm brown, mixed from Burnt Sienna, Rose Madder, and Cobalt Blue, softened and lightened with Yellow Ochre.

By painting into the wet finished greens of the trees, the shadow color picks up some of the colors underneath and becomes enriched. Outdoor painting, with its variety of forms, is greatly simplified by using a leading shadow color.

The same principle can be applied with equal success in figure and portrait painting. With more experience and skill, stronger colors can be set into the shadow tone to enrich a painting.

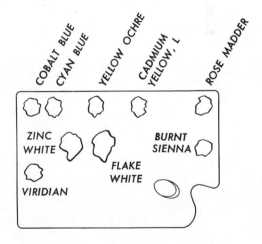

The diffused light in this painting is rendered in low-colored blues, blue-grays and gray-greens, in soft relationship to each other.

In the top left-hand corner, some blue sky is seen. The general color tone of the sky and the clouds is Cobalt Blue, white, and Rose Madder, warmed up with Yellow Ochre. The cloud to the left is brightened with a small touch of Cadmium Yellow, light.

The hills along the horizon are outlined and modeled in the shadow color over soft blues and violets.

The allover color of the verdure is painted from two separate mixtures of green which were made up on the palette. One mixture, for the darkest green, was made from Cyan Blue and Ochre; the middle shade, a warmer green, was made from Viridian, Ochre, and a little Cadmium Yellow.

Small variations in these greens, made by adding Cobalt Blue, Ochre, or Cadmium Yellow, and in some places Viridian, lend a feeling of lightness to the scene.

The use of such pre-mixed colors in distinctive tones of shadow, middle tone, and one for the general light, is generally helpful.

The sloping ground on each side of the middle distance, covered with sun-browned grass, and the grain field in the foreground are both painted in tones of rose grays with softer or stronger touches of ochre.

The canvas priming seen on each edge of the foreground is a cold gray.

Medium #1 slightly thinned with additional turpentine was used to control the color scheme. Flat sable hair brushes were the principal brushes used.

MODEL WITH WHITE SCARF

The painting shown here is a study of a professional model.

The palette is limited to four colors and white: Rose Madder, Venetian Red, Yellow Ochre, and a warm greenish-brown mixture of Yellow Ochre and black.

The painting surface is a square of bookbinders' hard cover-board, sized with glue and primed with white lead.

The study was painted directly, without any previously drawn lines.

The brown, made deeper with Rose Madder, outlines the features, and is used for the deep darkness in the background. The same color is used for the folds in the scarf and, deepened, for the eyes and nostrils.

The light and shadow forms in the background on each side of the face were laid in with the palette knife. The warmed-up light, to the right, is Venetian Red and Yellow Ochre loosely pressed down with the knife.

The white of the scarf is warmed up with light tones of Ochre and Venetian Red, while in the shadow, cool tones of Rose are added.

The light over the figure is painted in white, Ochre, and Venetian Red, cooler over the face.

The fairly flat modeling of the shadow in the face has ochre and brown as a warm reflected tone.

Middle shadows for the rosy cheeks and lips are painted in shades of rose-white.

Over the rounding of the shoulder to the right, a cold optic light contrasts against the deep warm shadow over the body. The total impression of the study is a cool silvery variation of painting in cold and warm.

Slightly warmer light at the bottom and increasing cooler tones upwards end abruptly against the scarf, and are repeated on the top of the head.

The model was sitting below eye level and is seen from above.

Quickly painted studies done without any previous drawing, such as this one, are invaluable aids in learning to paint in oils.

TONAL PAINTING.

The study shown here illustrates tonal painting in a gray-brown transparent color tone made from a mixture of Burnt Sienna, viridian, and a small amount of crimson with white lead.

The #2 medium was the only thinner used. Ink-drawing on a hard, white lead ground, helped to establish the areas of light and shadow.

For the purpose of strong contrasts a subject in lamp light was selected.

Only two colors were painted into the wet tonal color—Cadmium Yellow, light, with white, and a strong purple-black of crimson mixed with Ultramarine Blue.

Straight covering with the tonal color was followed by wiping out areas of light with a rag. Softening up of such places with a brush dipped in turpentine makes the rag wiping more effective and easier. In this fashion a wiped middle tone was quickly set out in all the lighted places. The tonal color, employed again over the darker areas, left a deeper shade of the same color, making the use of the purple-black necessary only in the darkest parts.

At first the light—yellow—was laid in with a soft brush in flat painting, leaving enough of the middle tone to be effective in the modeling of the shadow. The drawing and setting in of the deepest darks left only some highlighting and a necessary glint here and there to complete the painting.

After some practice of tonal painting the student will naturally begin to add several brighter colors. Experimenting with this method will add greatly to his knowledge of painting.

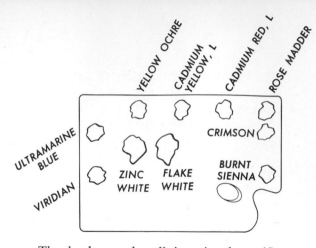

MURAL PAINTER

In the painting shown here, light thin yellow was laid as an allover undertoning over a drawing made with a medium hard pencil.

General drawing was done in light Rose Madder with a lettering brush into the wet yellow. The shadows on the body are indicated in the same color, in light shades and accents. Depth and shadow is similarly shown in all parts of the painting.

The pants, painting paraphernalia, and floor are drawn in heavier lines and darker shadows, also in the Rose Madder color with a slight amount of Flake White for painting quality. In general, this white is always added to Rose Madder and Alizarin Crimson as a precaution against cracking, especially in heavier coatings.

This method of undercoating in a specific color, such as light yellow, will hold together the total effect of luminous warm light over the entire surface of a painting.

Artificial light, which is usually necessary in mural painting, became the main feature in this picture.

The background wall is painted a trifle more golden in color with a semi-transparent mixture of white, Ochre, and Cadmium Yellow, light, in uneven brush strokes.

A light form behind the painter is "spared out" in the yellow, and painted a cool, light blue. The beginning of the mural—the leg of a figure to the left—has tones of red, gray, and ochre.

The head, arms, and the back are lightly modeled in thin shades of Cadmium Red and Yellow Ochre, leaving the lighter, cooler shadows alone, with only a few darker places set in with sienna. Sienna also models the hair, deepened with purple-blue.

The blue jeans were first painted realistically in Ultramarine Blue and white, and then the color was scraped down to a thin transparency. Shadows in a darker blue, and an occasional contour have accents of rose and viridian. The light areas are finished in a lighter blue, with scraped-in highlights on the left leg of the jeans, and in the ornaments of the light-colored belt.

The paint pots, palette, and water pail are painted simply, in cold and warm shades of blue. For the cooler, darker shades over the body, the warm, lighter ochre is matched with the sienna-brown and rose-gray, which models the musculature of the back.

The rose-gray was also repeated in the wooden box and the floor boards.

Two pencil drawings, made years ago on the spot, were used for this painting.

Every epoch in painting history has left us detail drawings by painters. Nothing was left to guesswork—not an ear, a hand, a turn of a head. With the support from his detailed drawings, the painter could proceed with certainty and speed.

CLOUDBURST OVER HOPI LAND

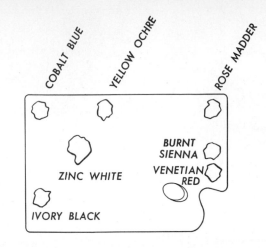

In this picture an old Hopi Indian village is seen against a rainstorm moving toward the site.

The houses stand out in a light ochre color. Still receiving some sunlight, they are in sharply defined relief against the blue-black downpour which hangs, curtain-like, from the storm clouds.

Fast and furious rainstorms like the one shown here are typical of the Arizona desert. The sun shining on both sides of the cloudburst makes it a spectacular sight, at a safe distance. Such subjects, of course, are not suitable for leisurely sketching. At most, one is able to catch the essentials before the subject has changed completely.

The color of the desert floor is a gray-yellow in many values, shifting from ochre to gray-brown. Only local colors of stone and sand show up under the overcast sky.

A lifeless gray shadow barely succeeds in giving form to the stones, cacti, and folds in the ground.

The only brilliant color in the scene is the sunlight divided by the curtain of rain. Light Cadmium Yellow, and pale values of Rose Madder are set off against the blue-black rain, pro-

viding almost the only direct contrast in the picture.

The dry transparent atmosphere of the desert is of little help in creating distance in painting—in rendering foreground, middle distance, and far distance. The noon sun with its short shadows, and the glaring light over the scenery, decolorizes and distorts what was seen earlier in the morning light. The evening dyes the hills and the shadows in the terrain in deep blue-violet and purple. The sunrise, an explosion of color, turns the grays and ochre of the stone landscape into gold and many shades of blue.

Painting this ever-changing light over the desert is a challenge to even the most determined painter with the speediest brush.

TREES IN BLOOM, SEASHORE

This painting shows how a small canvas (8⅞ by 16⅞ inches) may seem to take on mural proportions. The color is juxtaposed to simplify foreground, middle ground, and sky in such a way that perspectiveless depth is created.

The vertical forms of the tree trunks heighten the feeling of the endless sky. The stylized leafy trees and blossoms divide the greens into cold and warm above the horizon.

Underneath, the dark blue open sea spreads out as a cool backdrop for the bushes and grass in the foreground.

The lightest, warm colors are reserved for the sunlight over walks, and the grass and bushes to the left. On the right side cool blueish light is reflected over the grass.

Two low clumps of bushes in the golden colors of the morning light are set against the blue sea.

Left of center, a light blue cloud bank moves away, connecting the blue of the sea with the blue mist at the top of the sky.

Ornamental detail, such as the leafy trees and blossoming bushes, add interest to the painting. The green leaves are painted in dots and dabs, which softens severe stylization.

A quiet design of mural quality calls for

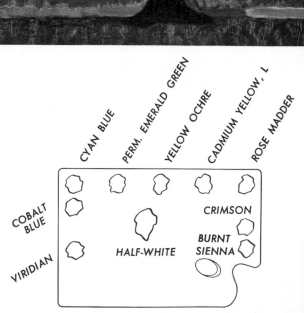

simple ornamentation and color, and the appropriate introduction of decoration, in contrast to the strident harshness of many modern pictures.

LANDSCAPE IN KNIFE PAINTING

Exercises in knife painting, such as the landscape shown here, contribute greatly to the development of a personal style of painting. When the painter is released from the tightening limitations of line, shading, and meticulous modeling, a more personal handling of the

206

tools and color is almost certain to emerge.

Knife painting does a great deal to remove the fear of being inaccurate in some detail, and it will not tolerate vagueness. It develops resourcefulness and boldness in applying paint to canvas. The lessons learned from it are automatically carried over into brush techniques.

Masonite panels are excellent painting surfaces for knife paintings. Glue size is applied to both sides; the primer is commercial white lead.

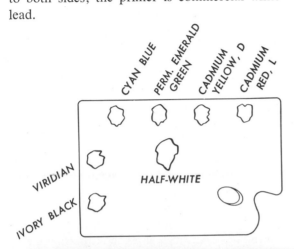

In the landscape shown here the sky, in black and white, is scraped down to a thin layer of pearly gray. A soft red and on the left a light green are scraped into the pearl-hued gray. In the center a white cloud is painted against a pink area. Dark gray clouds in black and white on each side almost dominate the painting. The darkest colors are the blue-black cloud shadows over the mountains. The dark forest greens along the mountain skyline are viridian blue-greens; the warmer greens contain Cadmium Yellow, deep.

Below the black shadow the same colors are repeated—dark warm greens over lighter blues and blue-greens.

Small, brilliant flecks of bright red are set into the green with the edge of the knife to simulate light on top of the taller trees. This red contrast makes itself felt in the whole color scheme.

On the shore of the Cyan Blue-black lake, two smaller trees are seen in a soft yellow light, with Permanent Emerald Green and blue-green shadows.

Soft, yellow-white Permanent Emerald Green grass and darker bushes fill out the foreground, effectively set off against the black reflections in the water.

The medium used in this knife painting was the heavier, more viscous #3. The size of the Masonite panel is 5¾ inches high and 8⅛ inches long.

Painting on small size boards or canvases is invaluable for on-the-spot painting. The sketch concentrated within a small format becomes homogeneous and rich in color.

PLASTER MIXING

This picture is painted from one of many sketches I made in working areas of buildings under construction. The plaster mixer is working up batches of fresco mortar in a ground floor area. The two light places in the upper left corner are parts of a bare brick wall. The cold black underneath, the warmer black strip behind the scaffold, and the colder one around the window are areas of black waterproofing.

The light yellow in the fresh lumber of the scaffold has dark, warm shadows. The scaffold, standing inside the window, contrasts with the light blue sky. Fresh lumber in the same colors, to the right, contrasts with the purple-black in the wall.

Two mortar mixing boxes stand in front of the scaffold and the lumber. Over to the extreme right there is an empty lime barrel, filled with water; dark gray and sienna shadows shape its form.

In the middle ground to the left, sunlight over pieces of lumber repeats the scaffolding color, linking the background with the foreground. Otherwise, the allover tone of the ground is a dusty, light, cool gray. The heavy shadow under the figure is blue-red, sharper blue inside, and this becomes the darkest, coldest color tone in the picture.

Behind the mixer the water bucket is blue-green in the light, and warm sienna in the half-light—an effective contrast to the purplish shadow. Inside the box is the cool color of the mortar in cooler and warmer reflective light. On the opposite sides of the box the shadow is

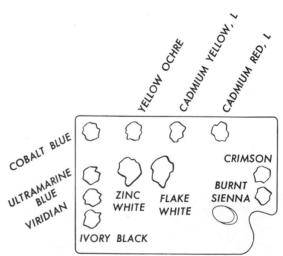

greenish-blue; the half-shadows are a little warmer brown. Lime-white is smeared over the box edges. This is the general color tone of a building interior under construction.

The man mixing the plaster is set in against this background. With his shirt and pants smeared with lime and plaster, and the ever-present dust, he becomes part of the general color of the working space. The general tone over the shirt is a mixture of cooler and warmer blue grays. Strong dark optic blue is reflected on the back of the pants. Wrinkles and folds in the shirt have shades of cooler and warmer reflections from the purple shadow in which the figure is standing. The sienna belt and deep sienna shadows in the folds of the pants bring out the modeling in sharp relief. Tan cotton gloves cover the hands, a "give-away" white cap, advertising lime, covers the head. The face and neck are sunburnt to a reddish brown.

The underlying idea of the shifting light is to establish contrasts in cool and warm everywhere. Soft light over dusty grays contrasts with brick red and black. The blue sky is in simultaneous contrast with the yellow in the fresh lumber, and in between, the blues, greens, and blue-greens oppose the warm sienna and black. Sharply contrasted chiaroscuro builds the color in cold and warm into well-defined sculptural form.

THE BURNING OF JUDAS

The Burning of Judas depicts the finale of the Jaqui Indians' Passion drama which I happened to see in Arizona.

The play was staged outdoors in the sunlight, with native costumes and scenery. It was fantastic, but always serious and dignified.

The top of a post driven into the ground carried a wooden image, the head of Judas, which was strangely modern in design and feeling. Below, nailed to the post, was a crossbar forming the arms, which held up the garments and gave shape to the figure. At the end of the drama props used by the players, such as masks and weapons, were piled up on the ground around the post. The burning of the pile is the climax, highlighting the spectacle. Before disintegrating, the grim faces of the masks seem to be thrown into convulsions as they are licked by the flames.

The deep blue sky, hot sand, and purple-blue shadows are the effective ingredients of the setting.

After the drama was over and I had left the scene, I made memory sketches and notes about colors and conditions. From these the composition for the painting was worked out.

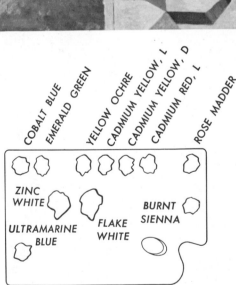

The picture is painted in opaque oil colors thinned sparingly with the #2 medium.

The design on top of the post and the post itself are gray-black in color. The garments, also in dark-gray ash-color, are ablaze; the tongues of fire leaping over them are painted in yellow-orange and in hues of Cadmium Red and Rose Madder. The piled-up masks and weapons, shown burning below, are painted in blue-green, Permanent Emerald Green, red and purple.

The burnt-out objects in ash colors and black have a functional purpose in the painting. The gray and the black are necessary to subdue the stronger colors, particularly in such a narrow area. Small bits of white among the bright hues emphasize these stronger colors in their true values of light and dark.

Predominating colors in the tonality are the black-violet and purplish blues and the contrasting dark red and orange-yellow.

The picture is 54 inches high and 34 inches wide, painted on linen with a medium-rough weave.

FLOWERING MAGNOLIA

Blossoms in shades of Rose Madder completely dominate the color scheme in this painting of a yard where a gnarled tree stands. The ochrish pink-white blossoms in the background serve nicely as restful passages.

Light spring green trees further back create the distance beyond the background houses in the center. Still further back, dark blue-green pines close the view to the left, and a dark blue-green maple closes it to the right. Viridian, Yellow Ochre, and Ultramarine Blue in these two dark blue-greens have a stabilizing influence on the mass of rose color.

The houses at the left are painted in cool shades of red-gray; the Cadmium Red and Cobalt Blue walls and Venetian Red-gray roofs act as another set of stabilizing intervals. The two houses in the center are painted in brighter red-grays, and the house at the extreme right has ochre-colored walls and a red roof. Below, at the right, a dull green shanty with a rust-red roof leans toward the center. In front of it are flowering bushes painted in light and deep Cadmium Yellows.

A thick hedge in dark green and blue shadow colors cuts off the foreground from the middle ground. Cold shadows thrown by the hedge over the cement sidewalk are forms drawn in perspective for depth. Their red-blue color is in direct contrast to the yellow tree.

The weathered white picket fence ties up the gray-white color of falling flower petals strewn over the back yard with the cold colors of the houses behind the fence.

The cold, light-blue of the morning sky provides the strongest contrast and is a color constant which makes itself felt in every part of the picture.

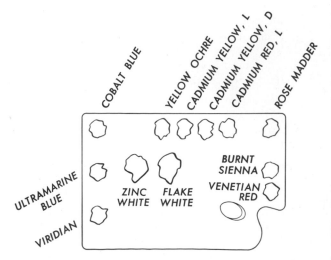

SUMMER EVENING

This picture features flat painting in cold and warm, and geometrical forms of houses contrasted against round forms of trees.

The forms, first outlined in Rose Madder, have a light undertone of light Cadmium Yellow painted over them. The center group of houses is painted in lavender. The walls of the two lower buildings are in red; the stone wall which divides the foreground and the background is painted in the same color.

The round forms of the trees reaching over the horizon have a dark warm green painted out flat over them. The color is scraped to make the tone light and semi-transparent. Deeper, cooler, viridian-blue shadows, warmed up with Cadmium Yellow, deep, and some ochre, are set

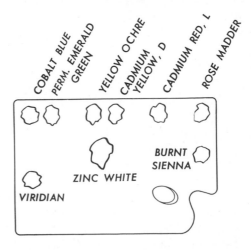

into the scraped color. Rose Madder is used as a contour-like shadow only in the deepest, darkest shadows.

211

The trees on the other side of the stone wall have the same colors in darker, warmer variations produced by deep Cadmium Yellow and Yellow Ochre.

In front of the long wall, three trees are painted in cool gray-blue greens and a light ochrish-green shaded with blue. Purple shadows underneath the sienna tree trunks bring out folds and irregularities of the ground.

Orange-yellow, reflected from the last light of the sunset sky, connects the upper and lower parts of the picture, and draws the colors together into a balanced tonality. In close harmony with the orange are the cold Permanent Emerald Green, blue-green and lavender, which complete the structural design of the foreground.

A horizon of light-blue mountains in the far distance is painted in a light tone to relieve the dark silhouettes. Afterglow from the setting sun is applied with Cadmium Red, light, and some Cadmium Yellow, deep, in loosely drawn contours and accents around the forms of the trees.

The same red appears in the houses, edging the gables; mixed with white, it becomes a lighter bright red of evening light reflected over the walls.

The transparent luminosity of a summer evening scene such as this one can be captured only if the utmost care is taken to paint in scrupulously clean colors.

A full-color reproduction of this painting will be found in the color spread.

STILL LIFE

If you are discouraged with a painting that you are working on, the best remedy is to leave it alone for the time being. When you reach such an impasse, try setting up and painting a still life. This often helps to solve problems that seem hopeless. Then when you take up the first painting again you will see it with fresh eyes and probably finish it easily. Besides, I want to point out once more that doing still life teaches technique faster than any other kind of painting.

The still life illustrated here was arranged as a compact composition set up against a dark red curtain beside a window. Painting of this luminous darkness began at the left side, using Crimson. Darker shadows in the folds of the material were set in with Rose Madder, deepened at the right side with Sienna. Transparent stripes in the folds to the left were lifted out by rubbing with a brush dipped in turpentine, then covered again with thin blue—a simple way to relieve the red monotony and tie the color to the cool light over the red objects in front.

The cold light over the grayish, off-white tablecloth changes the shadows to a greenish warm gray made of Ochre and Cobalt Blue, deepened with red. In the light over the table top, the off-white was made cooler by using black and white in a light mixture. Folds, formed by painting blue-gray light and deep shadows, enliven the shadow over the tablecloth in the foreground.

The pewter plate was painted in Ivory Black and white mixed to a gray. The left side was warmed up with Ochre. The edge of the plate outside the table was drawn in a blue-gray contour.

Stiff half-white and Medium #2 were used sparingly to thin the colors, when necessary, to make them paintable.

The beauty of fresh bread, the hard shiny crust, the soft inside in color tones of gold, is a favorite still-life motif. Bread is a symbol that means life itself to people in every country.

In this picture a cut loaf of Italian bread is featured. The ornamental cuts in the crust were painted in Ochre. The warmer, richer tonalities of the crust, in Ochre and Burnt Sienna, were made cooler in the light with white and more Sienna. The left end was modeled in warmer, deeper shades of Sienna and deep Cadmium Yellow. Cool highlights were painted in, and a sharp glint in two places completed the full modeling of this form.

Second in importance in the warm tonality is the green pepper. Warm green, the basic color of the pepper, was mixed from white, Cyan Blue, Ochre, and Cadmium Yellow, deep—the essential colors to produce this particular green. For modeling the light over the rounded folds of the pepper, more of the Cyan Blue was added. The shadow rounded out the form in full relief. White, shiny highlights, and a brown center were the finishing touches.

A cube of cheese with a bright red outer covering was placed close to the pepper. The

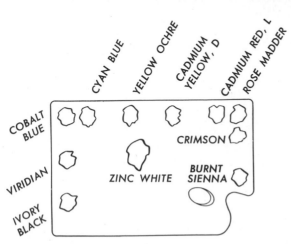

COBALT BLUE

CYAN BLUE   YELLOW OCHRE   CADMIUM YELLOW, D   CADMIUM RED, L   ROSE MADDER

CRIMSON

VIRIDIAN   ZINC WHITE   BURNT SIENNA

IVORY BLACK

the cold rose-red. The cold red of the cheese-covering functions as a balance, harmonizing the red elements in the painting.

The red onion and the deep-colored avocado that dominate the arrangement on the pewter plate also counterbalance the red background. The onion was painted in local color of Crimson and modeled in deeper rose and Cadmium Red. On the cooler side it has half-lights and highlighting in light shades of Cyan Blue and white. The characteristic lines, pulled together in the top center, were drawn in the darker red of the shadow. The light, bluish optic light on the side centered the red onion in a dominating position.

Dominating in a dark deep color, the avocado with its rough skin made a welcome contrast against the many smooth surfaces in the

covering was shaded in Rose Madder and white over the top; the shadow side was deepened in darker rose and red. On the cut side, the light yellow color of the cheese itself contrasted with

painting. It was stippled in blue-green, white, Cobalt, and Viridian on the light side. The shadow, in pure Rose Madder, Viridian and Cyan Blue, was reflected into the pewter.

Similar mirror reflections from each object's own local color made a rich variety of grays on the pewter plate—toward the right side in the cooler light over the table the grays are slightly bluer in tone.

The dark red of the background seen through the wine glass was made a shade bluer to give the glass its "glass hard" quality. White added to this color gave the same feeling of hard surface to the light on the rim and the reflections inside the glass. The golden-orange color of the sherry was made of Sienna and deep Cadmium Yellow, with modeling in a deep tone of Rose Madder. A broad band of reflected light slanting down from the edge of the glass was painted in the same color of Rose, with red and white added. The wine surface and the light at the bottom show a clear strong orange. Shining yellow light on the right side and white light on the left shaped the form of the glass. On the base, white lights were painted into warm gray modeling, to finish the painting.

A full color reproduction of this painting will be found in the color spread.

Chapter 12

Master Palettes

The palettes given in this chapter are correct as far as I can determine.

Delacroix, throughout his long life, never ceased to devise new palettes with different combinations and mixtures of colors. He did not actually paint from these but used them as "range finders." He made color samples on canvas swatches; bundles of these swatches hung in his studio.

Delacroix set up and combined a new range of colors on his palette for each large work—mural, *plafond,* and so forth—as well as for each important easel painting.

As time went on his palettes became more and more complicated. The "round palette" he used for the ceiling of the Apollo Gallery in the Louvre had twenty-eight pure colors on the outer perimeter, and below, another twenty-five made from inter-mixtures of the pure colors!

In large-scale mural painting, the color mixtures are painted from color pots. Delacroix used his color pots systematically, like playing organ music in color tonalities. Nothing was overlooked. With all the complicated color tones checked and in order, he could make any necessary changes without losing control of the color scheme. Such was the work—carried out in enormous scale—of a master colorist.

The Delacroix palette described here was chosen because of its fairly limited range. An early palette, it is believed to be the same as the one used by Van Dyck. Delacroix used this palette for his Palais du Luxembourg murals. It had ten pure colors, and nine of the same colors mixed loosely with white.

Palette by Delacroix

The so-called Van Dyck palette by Delacroix had this range of pure colors:

White; Naples Yellow; Yellow Ochre; Vermilion; Ultramarine Blue; Viridian; Raw Sienna; Cork Black; Madder Lake; Van Dyck Brown.

The pure colors were set out along the edge of the palette. Below were the same colors, mixed—turned over once—with a dab of white.

Palette by Cezanne

Brilliant Yellow; Naples Yellow; Chrome Yellow; Yellow Ochre; Raw Sienna; Vermilion; Red Ochre; Burnt Sienna; Madder Lake; Carmine Lake (fine); Burnt Madder Lake; Veronese Green Earth; Viridian; Green Earth; Cobalt Blue; Ultramarine Blue; Prussian Blue; Peach Black; Cremnitz White; Zinc White.

Palette by Gauguin

Ultramarine Blue; Prussian Blue; Cobalt Blue; Chrome Yellow, light; Cadmium Yellow, light; Cadmium Yellow Lemon; Cadmium Yellow, deep; Golden Ochre; Yellow Ochre; Vermilion; Madder Lake; Carmine Lake (fine); Veronese Green Earth; Viridian; Green Earth; Cremnitz White; Zinc White.

The iron oxides in this palette were probably artificial Mars colors.

Palette by Matisse

This palette by Matisse was done for the magazine, *Formes*:

Cadmium Red, light; Cadmium Red, dark; Burnt Sienna; Raw Sienna; Venetian Red; Yellow Ochre; Cadmium Yellow, deep; Cadmium Yellow Lemon; Cadmium Yellow, pale; Strontium Yellow; Alizarin Madder; Cobalt Violet, light; Cobalt Violet, dark; Cobalt Blue; Ultramarine Blue; Compose Green #1; Compose Green #2 (Block X); Viridian; Ivory Black; Zinc White.

Palette by Zorn

Some of the finest paintings by Zorn were painted with these few colors:

Yellow Ochre; Vermilion; Ivory Black (perhaps also another warm black—Bone Black or a warm, mixed black); Cremnitz White; Zinc White.

Palette by Utrillo

This palette, shown in an exhibition, was limited to the following colors:

Ultramarine Blue; Viridian; Chrome Yellow; Yellow Ochre; Vermilion; Alizarin Crimson; White.

Utrillo also employed palettes set up with a wider range of colors.

Palette by Odilon Redon

In 1886 Redon gave us this palette of "good colors":

Cremnitz White; Mars Yellow; Golden Ochre; Italian Ochre; Antimony Yellow; Mars Orange; Burnt Sienna; Mars Rose; Red Ochre; Carmine; Mars Violet; Cobalt Violet; Ultramarine Blue; Viridian; Green Earth; Raw Umber; Peach Black; Naples Yellow; Vermilion.

Chapter 13

Out of the Author's Sketchbooks

These drawings from my sketchbooks illustrate the various types that can be done with different drawing implements.

Black drawing ink comes in a variety of makes, some thin and fluid, others dense and opaque.

Many implements are available for drawing and sketching, each with its own technique —dictated in part by its limitations and possibilities, and by the ingenuity of the user. I will discuss only a few direct techniques here.

A sketch, drawn with a few loose lines in a small pocket-size book, can be a delight. Drawn as fast as the pencil or pen can move, such a sketch can catch the essence of the scene—the quality that made us sketch it in the first place.

The two sketches on this page, one abstract, the other ornamental in feeling, were both drawn with a kitchen match dipped in India ink.

The two subjects are similar, but not identical. The sketches were drawn on the spot, directly and quickly, before there was too much change in the light.

The sketch on the left shows a low morning light, with heavy black shadows; the sunlight comes from the right background.

In the second sketch the light from the foreground at high noon floods the open background. Less heavy shadows and loosely drawn ornamentation keep the objects flat on the surface. Broad blacks are drawn in brush-like flat strokes with another match cut in a chisel point.

The resting hiker is drawn with a slender reed pen; the broader blacks are put in with a thick bamboo pen.

The sketch of the seated girl shows another style and materials. A lettering brush was used, with India Ink, on Japanese rice paper. This paper is very porous; the ink bleeds right through and any ink stroke remains. The paper is so thin it cannot be erased, and calls for a direct, sure, one-stroke method. Dexterity is needed; no fumbles are allowed in this medium. One mistake and you have to start over on a new piece of paper. This is good discipline, and much can be learned from it.

A good assortment of Japanese rice paper is carried by the Stevens-Nelson Paper Corp., 109 East 31st Street, New York 16, N.Y. However, you can also practice this technique on inexpensive tissue paper.

Conté sanguine sticks and pencils should also be tried. The red shade produced is very useful in figure and portrait sketching. The drawings of Watteau, Chardin and Boucher, and their contemporaries, show what can be done in this technique.

The Conté black crayon was masterfully used by Seurat. You will find its characteristic rich, deep-black tones in his famous drawings.

Cold and warm-toned sepia sticks or pencils are excellent for landscape sketching.

Another very interesting medium is the *Chinese Ink Stick*. This ink, in solid form, is ground by rubbing on a small basalt slab with water as the diluent. It produces beautiful gradations of gray, as well as rich blacks, and is properly used with the long, soft, sharply pointed Chinese brush.

The Chinese brush, a single-stroke instrument, requires considerable training to use effectively. It is advisable to wait until you have attained a fair degree of skill with India Ink and ordinary brushes before you tackle this exquisitely refined technique. It requires delicate control of the most wonderful of all tools, the human hand.

For further study of sketching materials and techniques, I refer you to the excellent *Course in Pencil Sketching* by Ernest W. Watson, *Pencil Drawing Step by Step* by Arthur L. Guptill, and *Pencil Techniques in Modern Design* by Atkin, Corbelletti, and Fiore, all published by Reinhold.

In summing up this *Course in Beginning Oil Painting* I would like to emphasize again the vital function of color in painting.

The color must express the full power of the artist's ability.

The color must fulfill all the demands of the subject and of the central theme.

Equal importance must be given to all parts of a picture so that they may contribute to the allover tonality and color harmony.

Sketches

Sketches

Sketches

Sketches

Sketches

Sketches